50 Hikes in Michigan's Upper Peninsula

To
South Haven
Boy Scout Troop #198.

Hit the trail!!

Thomas H. Funke

50 Hikes

In Michigan's Upper Peninsula

Walks, Hikes, & Backpacks from
Ironwood to St. Ignace

THOMAS FUNKE

The Countryman Press
Woodstock, Vermont

With time, access points may change, and trails, signs, and landmarks referred to in this book may be altered. If you find that such changes have occurred on the trails described in this book, please let the author and the publisher know so that corrections may be made in future editions. The author and publisher also welcome other comments and suggestions. Address all correspondence to:

50 Hikes Editor
The Countryman Press
P.O. Box 748
Woodstock, VT 05091

© 2008 by Thomas Funke

All rights reserved. No part of this book may be reproduced in any form or by any electronic or mechanical means, including information storage and retrieval systems, without permission in writing from the publisher, except by a reviewer, who may quote brief passages.

ISBN 978-0-88150-807-9

Text and cover design by Glenn Suokko
Composition by Desktop Services & Publishing, San Antonio, TX
Maps by Mapping Specialists Ltd., Madison, WI, © The Countryman Press
Cover and interior photographs by the author

Published by The Countryman Press, P.O. Box 748, Woodstock, Vermont 05091

Distributed by W.W. Norton & Company, Inc., 500 Fifth Avenue, New York, NY 10110

Printed in the United States of America

10 9 8 7 6 5 4 3 2 1

DEDICATION

To my parents, James and Johnell Funke, for encouraging me to play outdoors.

Acknowledgments

First and most importantly, I need to thank my wife Susan, not for the usual clichés, but for traveling with me to remote parts of the Upper Peninsula, camping days on end in a small tent, and for her perceptive insights on nearly all the trails in this book.

Along the way, we have interacted with many state and national forest, park, and wildlife service employees. These on-the-ground public servants were very helpful in answering our bevy of questions, but most importantly pointing us in the direction of the trailhead. There were many, and their help was greatly appreciated.

Inspiration came in the form of perspiration, through hiking the entire length of the Upper Peninsula. Along the way, I saw parts of the Upper Peninsula that most have never seen. Many of these areas are highlighted in this book. One particular North Country Trail volunteer, Rolfe Peterson, took my constructive criticisms of the Trapp Hills segment of the North Country Trail and put me to work helping maintain the trail over two successive Memorial Day weekends!

Many friends and family joined me on my quest, either to hike across the Upper Peninsula just for the company or to bring dearly needed supplies. They include Sylvia and Dan Miller, Shawn Miller, Belinda Miller, Kim Thomas, Jeff Funke, James Funke, Annie Davidson, Julie Funke, Misha Durocher, Don and Barb McWethy, Elisabeth Hunt, Kristi Pawlowski, and Paul and Kira Frederick.

I spent several days driving across the UP with Mike Boyce exploring all of the Michigan Audubon sanctuaries. Dana Richter was especially helpful with sites in the Keweenaw Peninsula.

Jason Gatz at the Map Room, Western Michigan University Waldo Library, allowed me to find every map I needed for this book.

Eric Larcinese proofed the complex geological information for accuracy.

50 Hikes in Michigan's Upper Peninsula at a Glance

HIKE	LOCATION
1. Alligator Eye	Copper Country
2. Bear Lake Trail	Copper Country
3. Cathedral and Memorial Loop Trails	Copper Country
4. Forest Trail	Copper Country
5. Greenstone Ridge–Rock Harbor Loop	Copper Country
6. Lake Bailey Wildlife Sanctuary	Copper Country
7. N Country Trail: Copper Peak to Mouth of Black River	Copper Country
8. West Short–East Shore Trails	Copper Country
9. Oren Krumm Nature Trail	Copper Country
10. Overlook Trail	Copper Country
11. Summit Peak Trail	Copper Country
12. Tip Trail	Iron Range
13. Beaver Lodge Trail	Iron Range
14. Bog Walk and Nature Trail	Iron Range
15. Cascade Falls Trail	Iron Range
16. Cedar River and Ridgewood Trails	Iron Range
17. Clark Lake Trail	Iron Range
18. Craig Lake Loop	Iron Range
19. Fumee Lake Loop	Iron Range
20. North Country Trail: Trapp Hills	Iron Range
21. Overlook Trail	Iron Range
22. River Trail	Iron Range
23. Shakespeare Trail	Iron Range
24. Songbird Trail	Land of Hiawatha
25. Rivermouth Trail	Land of Hiawatha

DISTANCE (in mi)	FAMILY FRIENDLY*	WHEELCHAIRS*	OVERLOOKS	WATERFALLS	CAMPING*	GEOLOGY*	INTERPRETIVE*	NOTES
1.0	2	0	★			★	★	Overlooks, Lake Gogebic
2.5	3	1			M			Flat and scenic woods walk
2.2	2	0						Old-growth white pines
2.0	3	1			M		★	Large black ash trees
37.9	B	0	★		B	★		Island wilderness
2.0	1	0	★					Rugged climb, expansive views
6.0	1	0		★	B	★		Rugged, several waterfalls
2.0	2	0		★	S	★		Rugged, several waterfalls
0.7	3	0	★			★		Geology, overlook
3.5	2	0	★					Rugged, expansive views
1.0	3	0	★			★	★	Tower, expansive views
0.8	3	1				★		Rocky Lake Superior shore
1.25	3	0			R		★	Interpretive trail
0.3	3	2					★	Interpretive trail, bog, beach
1.6	2	0	★	★		★		Waterfall, expansive views
2.2	3	1			M			Mature forest, beaches
8.2	1	0			B			Rugged wilderness trail, loons, eagles
7.5	1	0	★		B			Wilderness trail, moose, loons
4.9	3	1						Flat and easy hike, loons
34.1	B	0	★	★	B	★		Wilderness trail, views
1.4	3	0	★		M,R	★		History, mature cedar forest
3.8	3	0	★		M		VC	Overlooks, moose sightings
0.5	3	1					★	Landscaping, interpretives
2.0	3	0			R		★	Interactive and interpretive, birding
14.7	2	0	★	★	M,R			Views, possible moose sightings

50 Hikes in Michigan's Upper Peninsula at a Glance

HIKE	LOCATION
26. Blind Sucker River Pathway	Land of Hiawatha
27. Chippewa Trail	Land of Hiawatha
28. Gold, Red, and Blue Trails	Land of Hiawatha
29. Horseshoe Bay	Land of Hiawatha
30. Laughing Whitefish Falls	Land of Hiawatha
31. Mackinaw Island Loop	Land of Hiawatha
32. Park Hiking Trail	Land of Hiawatha
33. NCT: Deer Park–Mouth of Two Hearted River	Land of Hiawatha
34. Scott Point	Land of Hiawatha
35. Pine Ridge Nature Trail	Land of Hiawatha
36. Falls Trail (Upper to Lower Falls)	Land of Hiawatha
37. Whitefish Point	Land of Hiawatha
38. Maywood History Trail	Land of Hiawatha
39. Au Sable Light Station	Pictured Rocks
40. Chapel Falls Loop	Pictured Rocks
41. Grand Island Loop	Pictured Rocks
42. Grand Portal Point	Pictured Rocks
43. Lakeshore Trail	Pictured Rocks
44. Log Slide Overlook	Pictured Rocks
45. Miners Beach to Miners Castle	Pictured Rocks
46. Miners Falls	Pictured Rocks
47. Mosquito Falls and Beach Loop	Pictured Rocks
48. Munising Falls	Pictured Rocks
49. Grand Sable Falls	Pictured Rocks
50. Sand Point	Pictured Rocks

DISTANCE (in mi)	FAMILY FRIENDLY*	WHEELCHAIRS*	OVERLOOKS	WATERFALLS	CAMPING*	GEOLOGY	INTERPRETIVE*	NOTES
6.7	2	0	★		R			Wild walk along large wetland, dry forest, Lake Superior
1.3	3	1			M			Wild beach walk
2.4	3	0						Wild lake, beach, wildflowers
2.5	3	1			B			Wilderness beach
1.0	3	2		★		★		Waterfall, ferns
8.0	2	0	★			★	VC	Views, wildflowers, history
2.0	3	0			M			Wetlands, forest, Lake Superior beach
12.9	B	0			B,R			Wild walk along Lake Superior
1.5	3	1						Wilderness Beach, wildflowers
1.4	3	1					VC	Excellent birdwatching
4.3	2	0	★		M	★	★	Waterfalls, wildlife
1.0	3	2	★				VC	Excellent birdwatching
0.6	3	3			R		★	Interpretive history
2.4	3	2			R		VC	Lighthouse, history, shipwrecks
6.7	2	0	★	★	B	★		Waterfall, wild setting, Lake Superior beach
7.4	3	0	★		B	★	VC	Good example of second growth, cliffs
9.1	1	0	★		B	★		Cliffs, geology
42.4	B	0	★	★	B	★		Cliffs, geology, beach, boreal feel
0.4	3	3	★			★		Interpretives, expansive views
2.4	2	0	★			★		Geology, overlook, beach
1.2	3	0		★		★	★	Waterfall, interpretives
4.5	2	0	★	★	B	★		Waterfalls, wild setting, Lake Superior beach
0.4	3	3		★		★	VC	Waterfall, geology
2.4	3	2		★		★	VC	Waterfall, access to Lake Superior beach
0.5	3	3				★	★	Interpretive boardwalk

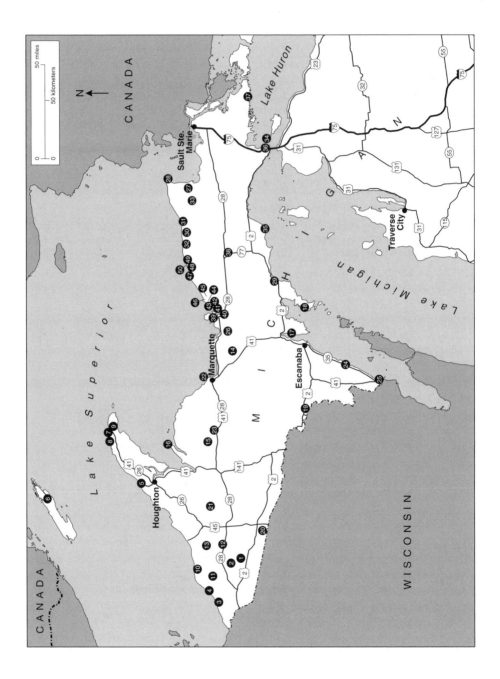

CANADA

Lake Superior

CANADA

Sault Ste.
Marie

Lake Huron

Houghton

Marquette

Escanaba

Traverse
City

Lake Michigan

M I C H I G A N

WISCONSIN

N

50 miles

50 kilometers

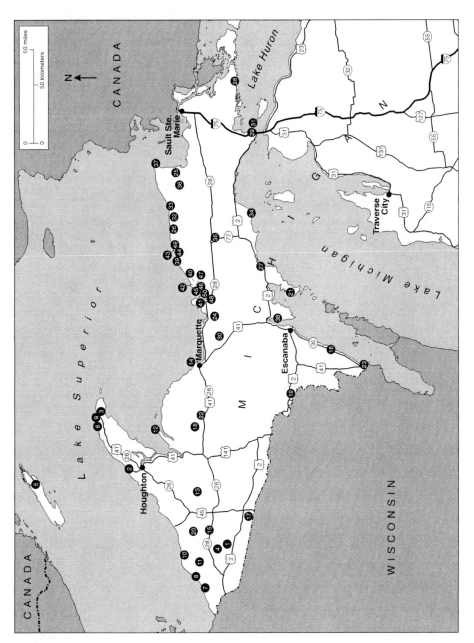

CONTENTS

Part IV Pictured Rocks

Introduction

My parents had had enough of suburbia. When I was at the tender age of eight, they moved our family to the seemingly remote countryside and set up camp in the sleepy farm community of Bangor, Michigan. This innocuous action on the part of my parents allowed me to spend an enormous amount of time outdoors as a child.

By this time in my life, I had been to Michigan's Upper Peninsula with my parents on various camping trips. Now, I had my own outdoor world all to myself—25 acres of fields, forests, and swamps.

Staying indoors was boring. We only had three television channels, and who wanted to watch soap operas all day? Instead, I clambered up trees, jumped in mud puddles, and explored for hours on end, until sundown, I became hungry, or I heard my parents honk the car horn from a half mile away.

Many of today's children spend too much of their time in organized sports, texting on their cell phones, or wasting away their childhoods playing video games.

As Richard Louv says (just wait, he will be famous someday), we need to prevent "nature deficit disorder." We can do so with our children and grandchildren by exploring Michigan's Upper Peninsula.

When most folks who live outside the Great Lake State hear the word "Michigan," they think of Detroit. If you want an urban experience, that is the place to be. If you are looking for a true nature experience, you need to drive the five hours north and cross the Mackinaw Bridge to the Upper Peninsula.

As soon as you cross the Big Mac, you discern right away that you have entered a wholly different world. The geology changes as there are rocks, outcroppings, and geological formations galore. The habitat changes noticeably. Even the weather feels different. You are in a truly wild place. Although the UP makes up one-third of Michigan's land mass, fewer than 3 percent of its residents live here.

Though it borders three of the Great Lakes, and has mountains, thousands of miles of rivers worth canoeing, and millions of acres of public land to travel around, it is the UP's hiking trails that truly envelop the visitor, offering even the most hardened suburbanite a wilderness experience.

It amazes me how many residents of Michigan's Lower Peninsula have never been across the Mackinaw Bridge and experienced the roar of the Tahquamenon, summited one of the numerous "mountains," or taken in a waterfall.

The area is grossly underrated for tourism—you could spend months in the UP and never see the same thing twice. It is truly an outdoor paradise.

GEOLOGY

As soon as you cross the Mackinaw Bridge, you have entered a different geological world. The Lower Peninsula and Upper Peninsula are as geologically different as they are geographically. The Lower Peninsula sits in what is called the Michigan Basin. Starting from the center of the peninsula, a set of concentric rings make their way outward in all directions. The rock formations in the center of the ring are a mere 60 million years old. Moving outward and northwestward, they become billions of years old in the Keweenaw.

Precambrian volcanic activity three billion years ago created the Canadian Shield, very dense igneous rocks that are the substrate for the western Upper Peninsula. The eastern Upper Peninsula and Lower Peninsula rocks are of sedimentary origin created during the Cambrian and Jurassic periods, making them 60 to 600 million years of age.

The Mackinaw Brecchia is the first geological formation witnessed as you drive north on I-75, just north of the Big Mac. The rocks only get more diverse and interesting as you head west.

The Precambrian Era encompasses 90 percent of all known geological time. It was during this time that the earth was cooling and forming the UP geology we enjoy today. This period started about five billion years ago, and only at 600 million years did a new era start, the Paleozoic. All time after the start of the Paleozoic is called the Cambrian.

The geology formed during the Precambrian has seen many changes over time. Volcanic activity, earthquakes, uplift, faults, and deformations have occurred and can be witnessed today. Most of Michigan's mineral resources, primarily copper and iron, find their origin in these rocks.

The Paleozoic's Devonian, Silurian, Ordovician, and Cambrian Periods (345–600 million years before the present) are when sedimentary rocks formed bedrock beneath the Lower Peninsula and the easternmost part of the Upper Peninsula. A notable exception is the Jacobsville Sandstone, which lies in a band forming the eastern part of the Keweenaw Peninsula and runs southwest towards Ironwood. This was created by an ancient river dumping sediment into a sea.

A "lost interval," as it is called, is the time period between the late Mississippian and the beginning of our current epoch, the Pleistocene, where there is no record of new bedrock being formed. The Pleistocene is known commonly as the Ice Age, and we are still in a time of glaciers scouring parts of the earth—although not a mile thick and covering the entire state of Michigan, as they did 30,000 years ago!

You can thank Canada for today's soil and for covering virtually all the bedrock in the Lower Peninsula, and most in the Upper Peninsula. This glacial till is hundreds of feet thick in places and is made up of all sizes of rocks, from microscopic silt particles to giant boulders the size of houses.

In many places in the Upper Peninsula, especially in the west, the bedrock is exposed or found just inches underfoot. The igneous rocks were very resistant to scouring by glaciers and in many places, too much topography to leave deposits of any great depth.

Even so, as you hike, the geology of the Upper Peninsula will influence every step you take. Learn the geological history of this region to enjoy your outings.

HUMAN HISTORY

Native Americans are thought to have first settled in Michigan's Upper Peninsula around the year 800 A.D., and were subsistence hunters on the plentiful game and fish resources. Tribes spoke various Algonquin languages and consisted of early Mishinimaki, Nocquet, and Menominee tribes.

The first European, Étienne Brûlé, a French explorer, crossed the St. Mary's River near what is now Sault Ste. Marie around 1618 in the never-ending quest to find the fabled Northwest Passage.

Sault Ste. Marie was settled about 1619 and is the second oldest city in the United

States after St. Augustine, Florida (settled in 1565). The French established missions and trading posts, until they forfeited these lands to the British after the French and Indian War in 1763.

The area known as the Upper Peninsula became part of territories claimed by the United States after the Treaty of Paris was signed in 1783. However, the British did not vacate the area until the Jay Treaty was signed in 1797. The fur trade dominated the economy of the area, and there was a major fur trading post at the strategically important Mackinaw Island. The American Fur Company operated there from 1808 until the 1830s.

The Michigan Territory, established in 1805, included only the easternmost part of the Upper Peninsula. The remainder was still part of the general territories of the United States. In 1819, the Michigan Territory was expanded to include the entire UP, all of Wisconsin, and a portion of Minnesota. If this had stuck, this book would have to be in three volumes!

Territorial Michigan, in laying the groundwork to become a state, made several proposals to specifically determine the official state lines. During this time, a conflict arose between Ohio and Michigan over what is known as the Toledo Strip. This strip, a narrow band of land containing Toledo, Ohio, stretched to the west, and was strategically important for whichever state was to govern it. The Maumee River empties into Lake Erie, through Toledo, and at this time in history this was a critical port for a new state trying to build its economy.

Ohio and Michigan had a tiff over this small, but very important, strip of land. In 1835, on the eve of Michigan becoming a state, this turned into what is known as the Toledo War. Statehood came to a standstill, as the constitutional convention convened to establish Michigan as a state. The convention would not accept Governor Steven Mason's idea to trade the vibrant and economically important port town of Toledo for the unknown and seemingly worthless Upper Peninsula.

A second convention was assembled, made up mostly of Mason supporters, and agreed to accept the UP in exchange for the Toledo Strip in December of 1836. The following month, the US Congress admitted Michigan as a state of the Union. In that day and age, Michigan was thought to have come out on the short end of the deal. Most thought the UP would remain a wilderness forever.

That all changed when copper and iron were discovered in the 1840s. Although not popular and precious minerals like gold and silver, copper and iron from the UP mines produced more wealth than the California Gold Rush. Once the locks in Sault Ste. Marie were built, along with developing rail and shipping routes, the extraction of these common elements became very profitable.

Through the 1860s, the mines in the Keweenaw supplied the majority of our growing country's demand for copper. The White Pine Mine was still the second largest producer of copper as recently as 1964, but finally closed in the mid 1990s.

In addition, the majority of our country's appetite for iron was supplied by UP mines through the 1890s. Iron peaked in the 1920s but is still is being mined in the Marquette area today.

The logging boom found its way to the UP in the 1880s, and by the 1920s, all but a few thousand acres of the majestic old growth adorning the landscape had been harvested. A few of your hikes will explore these uncut forests.

It was during these times that the region was flooded with immigrants, especially from Finland, although it was the Cornish who moved here first. Irish, Germans, and French Canadians were prevalent as well.

The UP is still home to the highest percentage of Finnish people outside of Europe. Michiganders even have a little fun with the dialectic mixing of these cultures with a bumper sticker you are bound to see: "Say yah to da UP, eh?"

Probably the biggest development in the past 50 years was the opening of the Mackinaw Bridge. Connecting two very different landmasses, this immense feat of engineering created a tourism boom in the UP that is still in force today. Instead of waiting hours to take a ferry from one side to the other, motorists can cross in less than ten minutes.

Today, 3 percent of Michigan's population lives in what amounts to one-third of the state's total land area. However, many temporary residents in the form of campers, anglers, hunters, hikers, and other lovers of the outdoors invade and take up habitation, even if only for a week of vacation. Native-born residents of the Upper Peninsula affectionately refer to themselves as "Yoopers," even before they would call themselves a Michigander! By the way, if you were born under the Mackinaw Bridge, you are lovingly called a "troll."

Part of today's culture involves some popular foods known (well, that's what the Yoopers want you to think, so just play along) only to the Upper Peninsula. The pasty (rhymes with nasty, but it really tastes great!), is sort of a combination between a turnover and a pot pie. Cornish miners brought this foodstuff with them, as it stayed warm when they were working underground. Many meats can be used to make this delicacy. Try to find one stuffed with potato sausage or cudighi, a spicy Italian meat.

Thimbleberry jams are popular, as this is a plant that produces plump berries but does not grow in the Lower Peninsula in enough quantity to harvest. Other favorite foods include maple syrup, lake trout, and whitefish. You should not have any problem finding these popular foods, as they are commonly available in grocery stores.

CLIMATE

Because it is surrounded by the Great Lakes on nearly all sides, Michigan's climate varies greatly in different parts of the state. To tell someone a statewide average snowfall, rainfall, temperature, or even percentage of sunshine is doing a disservice to most of the state, as there are wild fluctuations with all these parameters.

Lake Superior probably has the largest effect on climate, as it is larger and colder than Lakes Huron and Michigan. In addition, a majority of the shoreline of the UP is on Lake Superior, and prevailing winds are typically out of the west and northwest.

In the winter, this means snow—lots of snow. If you have spent any time in Detroit during the winter and think that the amount of snow in Motown is comparable to Copper Country, you had better pack some snowshoes. Where Detroit averages about 30–40 inches of snow a year, the community of Delaware in the Keweenaw averages more than four times that amount.

The Keweenaw, the Huron Mountains, and Pictured Rocks all are blasted with lake effect and winter storms to the tune of more than 100 inches of snow a year. However, Menominee averages less than 60 inches as there is little lake effect, and snow comes from continental weather systems blowing across the plains through Wisconsin. The general rule is that as you move south in the Upper Peninsula, there is less snow.

In spring, the Great Lakes keep most of the landscape cooler than more inland areas like Iron Mountain. This is the case as well in the summer—communities like Houghton, Marquette, Munising, and Paradise are considerably cooler than inland towns like Iron River.

Summers are mostly cool along the lakes and are more continental inland in places like Ironwood, Iron River, and Iron Mountain. It rarely gets above 90 degrees, even inland.

Fall can start early, leaves start to change in late August, and the first snow can fly even in late September. Fortunately, the lakes have a warming affect as they release all their stored heat to temper many of the lakeshore communities, keeping them warmer than some inland places.

Overall precipitation varies between 30 and 40 inches a year. Naturally, the total is closer to 40 inches in the areas with the heaviest snowfall along Lake Superior.

UP HIKING PRIMER

Folks living in the UP, Yoopers, joke that there are only two seasons: winter and mosquitoes. All joking aside, summers are mild and the winters can be horrendous. The best time of year, taking into consideration bugs and climate, is July through September. Winter lingers well into April, and some lakes do not even lose their ice until Memorial Day. I backpacked once in Pictured Rocks, and there was still ice floating in the water—in the middle of June!

Snow starts to fly in October and does not let up until the end of April. Another memorable camping experience was at Tahquamenon Falls State Park the last weekend in April, when there was still four feet of snow on the ground.

The geology of the UP is diverse and will have a significant impact on many of your expeditions. The western end of the UP was created by volcanic activity and is home to some of the oldest rocks on earth. Billions of years old, these rocks are very prevalent on nearly every trail in the western UP.

In the east, it is mostly glacial till covering the rocks, although there are several trails where roots and rocks rule. In the Pictured Rocks area, sandstone dominates, and as you will see, it can be dangerous to traipse along the edge of a precipice 100 feet above Lake Superior. For each trail, I will recommend footwear and give you an indication of the gradient.

Footwear

Backpacking boots: Of the highest quality, backpacking boots need to be sturdy, durable, and waterproof, and you should have a pair that is ankle high with a good sole with a steel shank if possible. These are recommended for longer excursions with a high concentration of roots and rocks.

Hiking boots: quality boots but not as tough as backpacking boots. These are recommended for shorter hikes that have roots and rocks to deal with.

Tennis shoes: These are recommended for flatter walks with trails with little or no roots and rocks.

Flip-flops: Flip-flops or sandals are suitable for flat, short walks with no roots or rocks.

Gradient

Extremely difficult: Only those persons with backcountry experience and proper equipment should attempt these trails. Expect steep climbs with elevation gains over 200 feet, roots, rocks, and difficult terrain.

Difficult: Any hills are less than 200 feet but more than 50 feet in elevation and not quite as steep. Again, one should be prepared and be able to negotiate some difficult terrain.

Moderate: Any hills to negotiate are less

than 50 feet in height, and most persons of average hiking skill should be able to hike them.

Easy: Few, if any climbs. Trail is mostly level.

Flat: No climbs but not quite wheelchair accessible.

Wheelchair accessible: Wheelchairs are encouraged and can use the trail.

The Ten Essentials

Every outdoorsperson should carry with them a small daypack with their ten essentials. Still, it astonishes me that 95 percent of the hikers I encounter do not have even a daypack. Most do not even carry water with them. It is amazing that we do not hear more stories about hapless hikers spending the night in the forest. Do not become a news story or a statistic. Develop a list of ten or more items that you always bring with you on an outdoor adventure. Mine are:

1. Map
2. Compass
3. Water
4. Extra food
5. Extra clothes (pullover, raingear)
6. Signal maker (whistle)
7. Knife
8. Fire starter
9. First aid kit
10. Flashlight

Some other items I bring are rope, duct tape, water filter, emergency blanket, bug dope, toilet paper, a shovel, and sunscreen.

Notice that I did not list a GPS unit or a cell phone. If you know how to use a map and compass, there is no need for a GPS. Cell phone coverage is spotty at best in the UP. Both require batteries, which can die on you. Both give the user a false sense of security. Spend time outdoors, experience nature, and learn the skills necessary to hike

and you will never need these gadgets.

Last, always, and I mean it, *always* leave your itinerary with someone. Let them know where you are going, your planned route (leave them a map!), and when you expect to be back. I always leave a time as well: if you have not heard from me by then, call the authorities, and I leave phone numbers to call. Thankfully, in all the years and thousands and thousands of miles I have hiked, only once have I not met my deadline.

Leave No Trace

Leave No Trace (LNT) ethics have been the mantra for many backpackers, but many day hikers have never heard of these seven easy rules of the trail. The basic premise is leaving the backcountry the way you found it. Here they are:

1. Plan ahead and prepare.
2. Travel and camp on durable surfaces.
3. Dispose of waste properly.
4. Leave what you find.
5. Minimize campfire impacts.
6. Respect wildlife.
7. Be considerate of other visitors.

Maps

You cannot use the excuse that a map does exist for your journey into Michigan's outdoors.

The United States Geological Survey (USGS) has created a series of 7.5-minute maps that cover the entire state of Michigan. Some trails are marked on these maps, most are not. Learn how to use a compass with these maps, and it will only make your hikes more enjoyable. Nothing is more satisfying than thinking that you are hopelessly lost, triangulating your position, locating yourself on the map, recognizing the landscape, then reconnoitering yourself back on track.

Most of the trails in this guide have a local map to which to refer. Nearly every trail less than 2 miles in length that has its own map will probably suffice. The longer the route, the more remote the area, and the less used the trail, the more you will want to bring a USGS 7.5 quadrangle with you.

Pets

Pets are commonplace in American families. Dogs are frequently seen traveling with their masters on vacations, and cats are traveling more and more every year. Our pets are great travel companions in our vehicles, in our campgrounds, and on the trail. However, there are times when pets are prohibited on a trail for various reasons, or there is a compelling reason not to bring them with you.

Bears, moose, and wolves are the wild residents in the north woods of the UP. A dog can be seen as a threat to these animals. In their natural habitat, you can never know if that particular bear, wolf, or moose is going to charge, run away, or attack you or your best friend. Although these incidents are rare, they do happen. Many dogs are killed in the UP each year by wolves.

Some landowners, especially the nature conservancies, prohibit pets because they can disrupt wildlife. Keep in mind, too, that your pet could pick up some nasty disease if it encounters the waste of any wild animal, especially other carnivores.

Therefore, each trail indicates whether pets are allowed. In some places, pets are illegal and the the law is enforced, such as in the Pictured Rocks National Lakeshore. In others, it is just not a good idea to take your dog into the woods as there is a greater possibility that you could encounter one of these wild animals. Enjoy your pets responsibly.

Amenities

Are there bathrooms? Can you camp?

These are legitimate questions when you are considering a hike in the woods, especially when you have children with you.

A rule of thumb: If your trail starts, ends, or traverses through a state park, or national or state forest campground, you are going to have potable water and a pit toilet. Other common facilities are camping, groceries, restaurants, and medical care. It is either feast or famine for many of your hikes, so prepare accordingly.

Hazards

No activity is free from risk, especially when you're traveling on foot in remote areas. Even if you become hopelessly lost, you are never more than 7 miles from a road in the UP. In addition, if you were careless and left your map at home, take a bearing (okay, you *did* bring a compass, right?) and you will come to a road in less than half a day.

Search and rescue personnel take lost hiker reports very seriously, so if you are late and nightfall is approaching, make a camp for the night. Water and heat are your two most important needs—therefore, resist the urge to eat unless you have a readily available supply of potable water, as digestion uses water to turn food into energy. You can go three weeks without food; you can last only three days without water. If you left your itinerary with someone and you stuck to your plan, you will be found in less than a day. If you are somehow off track, pull out the signal maker. Three successive blows on a whistle is a distress signal. If more than a day passes, start a small campfire and throw green leaves and needles on it. Nothing gets attention like a fire in the Upper Peninsula!

Next to getting lost, weather is your principal enemy. The time of year will determine which weather events you need to be prepared for. Another common adage we Michiganders use is: "If you don't like the weather, just wait 15 minutes and it will change." Fronts can and do move through quickly in all seasons.

Hypothermia is a real concern as the weather does change rapidly. You may an 80-degree day, then a front moves through soaking you with rain, and finally the temperature drops into the mid-40s . . . all within three hours. Raingear and a change of warm clothing stave off hypothermia and should be part of your daypack.

Summer brings thunderstorms and lightning, but the risk of tornadoes is very low. Using any trail during a thunderstorm is risky, especially if you are at a high elevation. Always get a weather report before leaving, and if you are caught in a storm, hunker down in a low area. In a forest, sit on top of your pack as far from tall trees as possible. In an open area, find a low spot and squat low to the ground, but do not lie on it. Do not resume hiking until a half hour after you have heard your last roll of thunder.

Fall brings stable weather, but snow squalls can occur as early as late September. If you are caught in a squall, get out to the trailhead as soon as possible while using and staying on the trail. If you are lost or cannot make it any farther, hunker down for the night by creating a shelter out of natural materials. Your chance of survival is much greater snuggled in leaf litter than it is wandering around.

Winters are very cold, but snowfall varies across the UP. Along Lake Superior, some communities get more than 200 inches of snow a year. Along the northern shore of Lake Michigan, it is more moderate with less than 100 inches in a winter season. All the trails described in this book are snowshoeable in the winter months, so use winter preparedness techniques when venturing out.

Spring is snowbound until late April or early May. Spring brings mosquitoes, blackflies, and no-see-ums, even when there is still snow on the ground. Again, snow is possible into mid-May, and there is the occasional threat of a thunderstorm.

Wildlife hazards include biting insects, which bug spray or clothing will cure. Ticks exist, but are not common in the UP. Stable or beach flies are a surprise to most non-Yoopers as they land on your legs, looking like an innocuous housefly, but bite like a horsefly, and are immune to DEET.

Many folks unfamiliar with wilderness are nervous about the presence of animals such as rattlesnakes, lynx, moose, bears, and wolves. You will probably never see a lynx or a wolf in your lifetime, and moose are extremely rare, except on Isle Royale. Since the black bear is aggressively hunted in Michigan, they are terrified of most humans and flee on sight. However, if you find yourself in the presence of a bear, especially a mother bear and her cubs, you need to take evasive action. The likelihood that she will attack is extremely remote; however, she could make a bluff charge in your direction to convince you to leave the area. If the bear does not see you, move on without drawing attention. If it does see you (they have poor eyesight, so she is smelling you), wave your arms and make some noise, like "Nice bear! I'm leaving now!" Walk backwards away from the bear, and all should be well. The more time you spend in the UP, the greater the chances you will see a bear.

There are no venomous snakes in the UP, no matter what anyone tells you. The only venom is from the countless spiders trying their hardest to eat all those mosquitoes and flies. Poison ivy and poison sumac are present in the UP, but very uncommon. Poison ivy grows in just about every terrestrial habitat, while poison sumac is found only in swamps. Learn how to identify these plants and how to treat yourself if infected with their oil. Poison oak does not grow in Michigan.

Forest fires occur nearly every year in the UP, although they tend to be very small and are put out quickly. The Sleeper Lake Fire of 2007 burned over 18,000 acres, reminding everyone that fire is a real and present danger. Thankfully, no one was hurt and very little property was destroyed.

Regions

I have divided the UP into four regions: Copper Country, Iron Range, Land of Hiawatha, and Pictured Rocks.

Copper Country is essentially the Keweenaw Peninsula, the Porkies, and eastern Gogebic County. This area is known for its great copper deposits, which have been mostly mined and could be found as wiring in your home. This area is where you find ancient mountains, which means roots and rocky footing, steep climbs, and sweeping views.

The Iron Range is the area east of the Copper Country over to the midpoint of the UP. This area is known for its iron deposits, which contributed greatly to the economy during the late 1800s, creating cities like Marquette. Not as mountainous, it is still rooty and rocky in areas.

The Land of Hiawatha is the eastern part of the UP, which is known for its pine forests, sandy soils, and extensive swamps. Trails are relatively flat but a few have some climbs and a rocky footing.

The Pictured Rocks section highlights trails in the Pictured Rocks National Lakeshore and Grand Island. Sandy footing is the norm, along with sandstone formations. Expect some varied topography and hardwood forests.

If I had to pick one trail in each region and take someone who has never been to the UP to give them a feel for this wonderful part of our state, I'd first visit the Estivant Pines Sanctuary to show them what the forests looked like before Europeans came and changed everything. Next stop would be Craig Lake State park for our best chance to see a moose, Michigan's largest animal. In the Pictured Rocks, I would venture around Grand Portal Point for the colors that Michigan provides in the water, rocks, and plants. Finally, I would spend an afternoon dodging roots and rocks between Upper and Lower Tahquamenon Falls to highlight our two most popular waterfalls.

I

Copper Country

1

Alligator Eye

Place: Ottawa National Forest

Total distance: 1 mile (round trip)

Hiking time: ½ hour

Gradient: Moderately difficult

High points: View of Lake Gogebic

Maps: USGS 7.5' Marshall Creek

*Amenities: Gogebic County Park,
Ontonagon County Park, and
Lake Gogebic State Park are nearby,
along with several lodging possibilities
and small markets.*

Footwear: Hiking boots

Pets: Yes

SUMMARY

Alligator Eye is easily accessed but not easily climbed.

This lump on the landscape is a remnant of a rugged ancient mountain that has eroded over the billion years or so since it was created. Most recently (geologically speaking) this area was eroded by glaciers and then covered with glacial till about 10,000 years ago.

Native Americans moved in soon after the last ice sheet vacated the area. The quartz found in the rock formations made for great cutting tools and arrow and spear points for hunting game in the area.

The Native Americans were probably also attracted to the fishery resources in Lake Gogebic. Sitting at 1,204 feet in elevation, covering 14,781 surface acres, and with a maximum depth of 37 feet and a shoreline 34 miles long, this lake is home to enormous numbers of walleye, smallmouth bass, and perch. The West Branch of the Ontonagon River drains the lake to the north.

Lake Gogebic was first opened to tourists in the summer of 1884, when the Milwaukee, Lake Shore & Western Railroad began providing rail service to the area. Travelers were attracted to a hotel and resort complex built at the south end of the lake. Not much has changed in attracting visitors to the area, because then, as now, the Upper Peninsula's largest freshwater lake, its clean air, and its excellent fisheries are still a major draw.

There is great debate about what exactly the word "Gogebic" means. The word is thought to be derived from the Chippewa

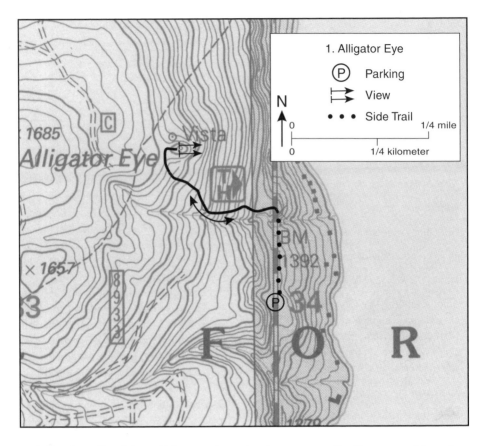

word *Akogib* or *Akogibing,* which may refer to someone, something, or somewhere. There are many claims about the origin and definition of the word. The debate has been going on for more than 100 years and is far from settled.

One local translation comes from a Chippewa word meaning "Where trout rising to the surface make rings on still waters." Since this is the largest lake in the Upper Peninsula and is known for its great walleye fishery, who could argue with that translation?

The first known attempt at finally getting to the origin of the word and its meaning was started in 1885, the same year the railroad came into the area, by the editor of the

local newspaper, the *Ontonagon Miner.* An editorial printed various meanings of the word Gogebic, including "green lake," "little fish," "place of the falling leaves," "porcupine lake," "bear in the water," and "body of water hanging on high." I think we can agree that the true origin and meaning of Gogebic are lost on the pages of time.

Surrounding the lake and Alligator Eye is the million-plus-acre Ottawa National Forest.

ACCESS

From Bergland, take M 28 west, then turn south on M 64. Two miles past Lake Gogebic State Park, look for trailhead markers. Parking is on the west side of the road, about 200 yards past the trailhead.

Overlooking Lake Gogebic

THE TRAIL

Alligator Eye is not so named because some unscrupulous pet owner dumped their Floridian reptile into the cruel waters of this Upper Peninsula lake. The name was derived from anglers on Lake Gogebic, who thought that the landscape resembled a large alligator, with the summit serving as its eye.

The trailhead is marked by a modest post with a hiker symbol. Start by climbing a wooden staircase into the hardwood forest dominated by sugar maple and white ash. Ground cover includes Solomon's seal and sarsaparilla, while young red maples make up the bulk of the remaining vegetation.

Rooty and rocky, the trail follows a ravine on your left for 0.2 mile. A bench is appropriately situated before your steepest climb.

Veer to the right and take a gentle climb, turning left in another 100 yards. As the trail turns left, your steep climb up the backside of the overlook begins. Climb moderately 150 feet in elevation to an interpretive panel. From the interpretive panel, turn right, and go up about 30 feet more to the vista, which is at approximately 1,620 feet above sea level, about 300 feet above Lake Gogebic.

Your view is east, over Lake Gogebic, looking through a gap in the forest canopy.

2

Bear Lake Trail

Place: F.J. McLain State Park

Total distance: 2.5 miles

Hiking time: 1–2 hours

Gradient: Flat

High points: Bear Lake, beach walk, sunsets

Maps: USGS 7.5' Hancock; F.J. McLain State Park map

Amenities: Modern campground

Footwear: Tennis shoes

Pets: Prohibited on part of the trail

SUMMARY

This loop trail may start in a hectic campground; however, you will leave everyone behind after crossing M 203 into the woods and rambling along Bear Lake. In a maturing forest, your outing is on a wide, well-maintained path with some interpretive signs.

The trail will loop back across into the park, going between rental cabins and the beach. You will reenter the campground, and you have the option of walking the campground loop or finding one of the several staircases leading to the beach for a walk in the sand on the shore of Lake Superior.

ACCESS

From Hancock, take M 203 8 miles north, and the park entrance will be on the left. Check in at the contact station, turn left, and immediately park in the day use area.

THE TRAIL

Walk back up the entrance drive 0.2 mile, cross over M 203, and enter the woods, which are open to hunting. The wide, wood-chipped corridor contrasts nicely with the maturing paper birches and red oaks lining the trail. Carpeting the ground are winterberry and bracken ferns.

Winterberry, a member of the heath family, is a creeping evergreen plant. About 4 to 6 inches high, it can carpet forest floors with its shiny, green leaves and edible red berries. The best way to enjoy this fit-to-be-eaten forest treat is by picking a leaf and placing it

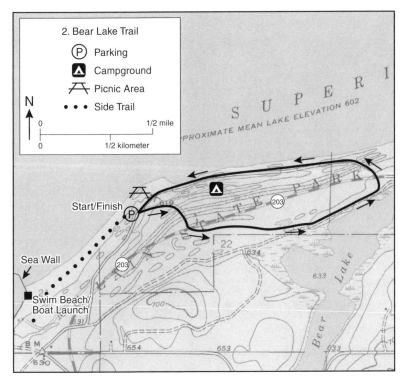

2. Bear Lake Trail

ⓟ Parking

△ Campground

⼌ Picnic Area

• • • Side Trail

N

0   1/2 mile

0   1/2 kilometer

Start/Finish

Sea Wall

Swim Beach/
Boat Launch

between your back teeth, gently chewing it every so often. If you are already chewing a piece of gum, break off a small piece to obtain the wintergreen flavor and it will turn green!

Parallel M 203 as it squeezes between this highway and Bear Lake and the wetland that surrounds it. For the next 0.2 mile, you are in a maturing mixed forest with the aforementioned hardwoods and some red and white pines thrown in for good measure.

Your footing is high and dry, but you will notice shrubby wetlands on your right. At the 1.0-mile mark is a bench where you can sit and look through an opening to Bear Lake. Along Lake Superior, this is a harbor of refuge for migrating waterfowl such as mergansers, loons, and ducks.

About 0.1 mile farther on, take a side trail and walk out onto an old dock, which is being overgrown with emerging plants like blue flag iris. Look for the white water lily floating on the surface in midsummer.

After the side trail, begin to turn northward toward the highway and cross M 203 at the 1.2-mile mark. You will leave the woodchips behind, and the habitat becomes more open with a well-used tread on the ground. At the 1.5-mile mark, you will enter the campground and be greeted by a sign indicating that you are entering a dog-free zone. This area hosts several mini-cabins, and you will stroll past these using the paved walkway 1 mile back toward the day use area.

At any time, you can use one of the several staircases leading to the shore for a beach walk if you desire. The beach is sandy and free of obstructions although it may have folks enjoying such activities as Frisbee or a pickup game of football.

Bear Lake Trail in F.J. McLain State Park

If you walk through the campground loop, you will notice that a number of campsites have fallen to the beach below. Erosion eliminated about 20 sites a number of years ago. Turning lemons into lemonade, park personnel installed numerous benches for walkers and campers alike to take in Lake Superior and its sunsets.

Entering the day use area, you can end your stroll here or continue along the beach, which is a little wilder and little used, all the way to a seawall and fishing pier.

3

Cathedral and Memorial Loop Trails

Place: Estivant Pines Sanctuary

Total distance: 2.2 miles

Hiking time: 1–2 hours

Gradient: Moderate

High points: Old-growth white pines, rare orchids, and other uncommon plants

Maps: Estivant Pines Sanctuary trail guide

Amenities: None

Footwear: Hiking boots

Pets: Yes

SUMMARY

Located near the tip of the Keweenaw Peninsula, Estivant Pines is a 500-acre sanctuary that has been pieced together over time to save large tracts of old-growth white pines.

There are two loops. The Cathedral Loop and the Memorial Grove Loop, when combined, make for a nice 2.2-mile walk that should take you less than two hours to explore. The terrain is infested with roots and rocks as the trail rolls over the landscape in the sanctuary. Both will give you a glimpse of what Michigan looked like before the lumber barons showed up in the late 1800s. There are several groves of old growth in the forest, left behind by loggers.

Edward Estivant, from Paris, first purchased this tract in 1861 during the copper rush, as part of a 2,400-acre plot. By 1900, only 750 acres of old growth remained. This tract stayed in the Estivant family until 1947, when it was acquired by a mining company. In 1968, the mining company was purchased by Universal Oil Company, and the logging of the old growth started again in 1970.

Locals rallied against the logging, but there was not much they could do short of purchasing the land holding these stately giants. That is what happened when the Michigan Nature Association procured this parcel three years later, establishing Estivant Pines Nature Sanctuary. Monies raised came from all parts of the state, as this was a special place worth saving.

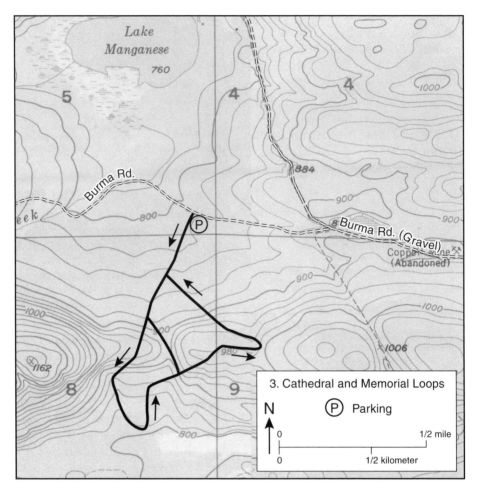

The story does not end there. A case of trespassing by logging occurred just to the west of the trailhead when 24 old-growth trees were cut. In the meantime, another adjacent owner considered cutting some of his old growth. The locals rallied, raising more monies to buy this land, adding 177 acres and an endowment that provides for maintenance.

Since then, more parcels have been added and the sanctuary is nearly 500 acres in size. Whenever an old-growth forest is saved, many other species sensitive to disruption are saved as well. Estivant Pines is known for its biological diversity—bring your identification guides and keep your eyes open for a wide variety of plants. Ferns include maidenhair, spleenwort, Braun's holly fern, rusty woodsia, and common polypody. Flowers include more than 12 species of orchids and some more common species such as large-leafed aster, Clintonia, bloodroot, pyrola, rose twisted stalk, and sarsaparilla.

ACCESS

From US 41 in Copper Harbor, turn right (east) at the flashing light. There should be a sign directing you to Estivant Pines at this

Boardwalk along trail

intersection. This road is paved for a short period, as it brings you through a private campground and resort. The road splits to the south (to your right) and turns to gravel. Follow the numerous signs for Estivant Pines, which is about 3 miles. Drive carefully on this road—it is rough, but passable even in small cars if care is exercised.

THE TRAIL

The trailhead includes a few parking spots and a kiosk describing the sanctuary's history and identifying the different loop trails.

When you set off on your way into the sanctuary, you would not think you are soon to be surrounded by majestic white pines, as it is young forest where you start. This is probably because the parking area for the sanctuary is on private property that was logged off in recent years.

Your footing can be soggy, which explains the planks neatly placed on the ground. Blue triangles lead the way up to your first intersection 0.2 mile into your jaunt. There is a YOU ARE HERE trail sign at the intersection of the Memorial Grove. You will eventually come out here at the end of your adventure.

Continue in a counterclockwise direction, uphill, into a mature white pine forest with the occasional large red pine. In another 0.2 mile, you will come to your second intersection, with another YOU ARE HERE sign. You will turn right, leaving the well-used and wide trail, and take the winding, root- and rock-covered trail into the mature forest.

Walking the Cathedral Loop, notice the ground covered in Clintonia. Masked by these two-leafed flowers are orchids, which are similar in appearance. Keep your flower guide handy, as there are hundreds of species of plants on the forest floor. This has remained a very diverse place, having not been disturbed since the glaciers retreated 10,000 years ago.

Roll over the landscape and you will need to watch the tops of your feet, as it is quite rooty and rocky. At 0.6 mile past the intersection, take a moment and look up and feel dwarfed by the massive, 4-foot-wide white and red pines. These giants of the woods remind us of what this area looked like before our ancestors removed these trees for lumber.

For the next 0.25 mile, walk through what is known as Cathedral Grove. Just after leaving this grove of massive trees, you will come to an intersection and another YOU ARE HERE sign. Continue in a counterclockwise direction, climbing up and down some short (less than 20 feet), but steep inclines and declines. As this is a nature sanctuary, be advised that there may be the occasional deadfall blocking your way. Beware, the deadfalls here can be 4 feet or more in height!

Enter another old-growth area, the Memorial Grove, at 0.4 mile past the intersection. The ground is still covered in all kinds of wildflowers, small shrubs, and emerging trees. The trail bends from eastward to the northwest as you move through this grove. You will come back to an intersection leading you to the parking area 0.4 mile after leaving this grove of old growth. Again, the trees are so large that you will probably find yourself at the intersection before realizing you have left the old growth. What a great feeling that is.

4

Forest Trail

Place: Lake Gogebic State Park

Total distance: 2 miles

Hiking time: 1–1½ hours

Gradient: Easy to moderate

High points: Large black ash trees, wildflowers, ferns, interpretive signs

Maps: USGS 7.5' Marshall Creek; Lake Gogebic State Park map

Amenities: Modern campground

Footwear: Tennis shoes

Pets: Not recommended

SUMMARY

In Michigan, there are several species of trees that never get large enough to wow the average nature enthusiast. Those familiar with the trees in the Great Lake State know that species such as blue beech, ironwood, and dogwoods never get much larger than the width of a forearm.

When Michigan was logged off at the turn of the last century, we lost the vast majority of our majestic trees that used to scrape across the sky. Most think of the stately white pine, probably the red pine, along with some oaks and maples when it comes to large trees.

But black ash?

We do not think of black ash as growing very large because most of us do not spend time walking in its preferred habitat: swamps.

The Forest Trail at Lake Gogebic State Park quietly hosts several splendid black ash trees, and a hiker does not have to trudge through waist-deep muck to see them. Although there are a couple of moist areas, these trees seem to flourish, surrounded by more typical western UP trees such as northern hemlock, yellow birch, and sugar maple. There is even the occasional basswood to keep a botanist honest in these thick and mature woods.

ACCESS

From Bergland, take M 28 west and turn south on M 64. Lake Gogebic State Park is on the east side of the road, well marked by signs. After the contact station, turn right and park at the far end of the day use area. Walk back toward the contact station, then

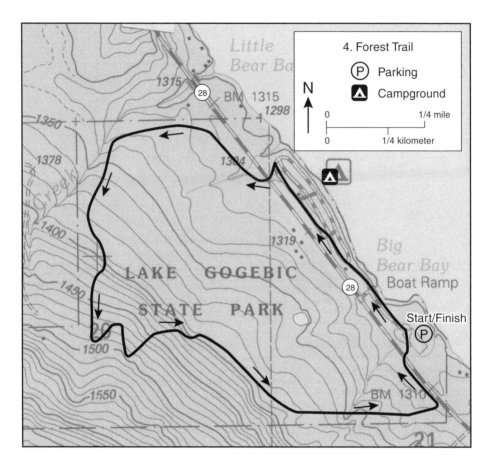

Little
Bear Ba

4. Forest Trail

Ⓟ Parking

🔺 Campground

N

0   1/4 mile
0   1/4 kilometer

BM 1315
1298

1315

28

1378

1384

1400

1319

Big
Bear Bay
Boat Ramp

LAKE   GOGEBIC

STATE   PARK

28

Start/Finish
Ⓟ

1450

1500

1550

BM 131

21

continue onto the western campground loop. The trail starts at site #36. You will end at the contact area near your vehicle.

TRAIL

On a busy summer day, your escapade will start by exposing you to a sea of humanity. Leave the contact area, the picnic tables, bathers, and playgrounds behind. Pass the contact station and dump station, and follow the campground's western loop past happy campers. The trailhead for the Forest Trail is clearly marked.

Squeeze between two campsites and within 100 yards, cross the lightly used

M 64. This is a loop trail, which will bring you back to the day use area. Almost as soon as you enter the woods, you will likely leave most of the park's users behind you, across the state highway.

Cross a gully and head northwest through a young forest dominated by sugar maples. Bend to the west and follow the northern boundary of the park. The forest takes on a mature composition as you start to climb uphill, and you may notice another gully holding Gillis Creek on your right.

Keep climbing gradually up the landscape and pass through stately hemlocks, yellow birches, and sugar maples. At the

The Forest Trail

0.5-mile mark, take a southward turn. The climb gets steeper, and you now parallel the western boundary of the park.

Ferns such as the maidenhair, oak, ostrich, sensitive, and woodfern predominate along this stretch of trail. At the 0.8-mile mark, make a hairpin turn as you bend back to the east, negotiating the southwest corner of the park. Start your gradual downhill descent while keeping your eye open for some upcoming large trees.

From the 1-mile mark to the highway crossing, there is the occasional large basswood and black ash. Basswood has heart-shaped leaves the size of your hand, making identification easy. Another key identifying feature is that some mature trees sport ten or more small sprouts around the base of the trunk. Sometimes called a "fairy's crown," these are indications of a past disturbance such as a fire or cutting.

The black ash also sprouts vigorously after being damaged. The leaves are compound, with seven to eleven leaflets. Native Americans used strips of this flexible wood for basket weaving, and today black ash is still highly sought after for this craft. The wood is pounded into thin sheets and then cut into strips.

Cross M 64 and walk north on the highway 0.1 mile and quickly jaunt over to the parking area to complete your hike.

5

Greenstone Ridge– Rock Harbor Loop

Place: Isle Royale National Park

Total distance: 37.9 miles

Hiking time: 6 days

Gradient: Difficult

High points: Roadless wilderness island ecosystem with moose, wolves.

Maps: USGS 7.5' Rock Harbor Lodge, Belle Harbor, McCargoe Cove, Mott Island, Lake Ritchie; National Park Service Isle Royale topographic map

Amenities: Lodge, store at trailhead.

Footwear: Backpacking boots

Pets: Prohibited and illegal

SUMMARY

"Wilderness."

The word evokes thoughts of wild animals living in wild places, free of human activities. Forty-five miles long and 7 miles wide, Isle Royale's thinly covered volcanic rock is home to animals that define wilderness: wolves, moose, loons, and well over one hundred species other of birds. One species that is notably absent? Humans. This is the second least-visited national park in the United States (after the National Park of American Samoa), with fewer than 20,000 visitors a year. Yellowstone receives more visitors on a busy summer day than Isle Royale does in a year.

Isle Royale is the only national park that completely shuts down at the end of its season. No humans are present for about half the year, leaving the island to the resident moose and wolves eking out their existence.

Although most human visitors to the island are of the backpacking variety, there are other ways to enjoy Isle Royale. Popular activities include canoeing, sea kayaking, scuba diving, and boating.

If you so choose, you can stay at the elegant and modern Rock Harbor Lodge.

If you plan to go, keep in mind that 130,000 acres of the over 500,000-acre wilderness is terrestrial, with limited services, and only at Rock Harbor and Windigo. Venture more than a quarter mile from either, and you are on your own.

A major attraction is the opportunity to see that symbol of wilderness, the wolf.

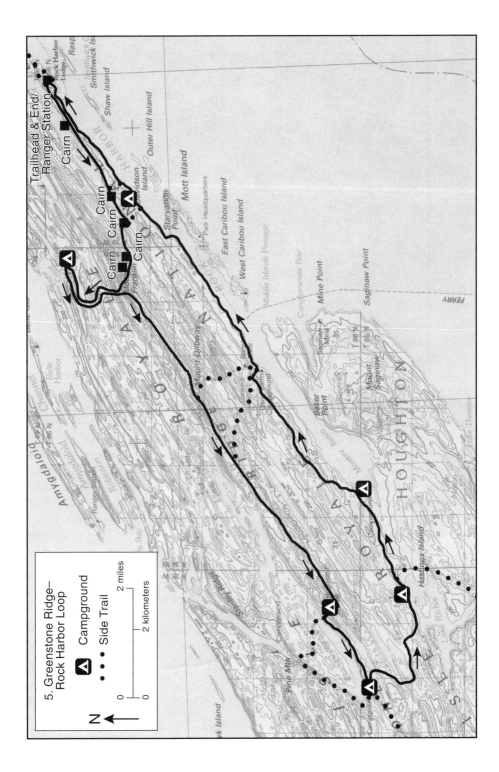

5. Greenstone Ridge—
Rock Harbor Loop

▲ Campground
•••• Side Trail

N

Trailhead & End/
Ranger Station

Cairn
Cairn
Cairn Cairn
Cairn Cairn
Franklin Cairn

Moose at Isle Royale National Park

Unfortunately, the vast majority of Isle Royale's visitors never spot this secretive animal. If you really want to see a wolf, you will need to get to the island when it first opens in mid-April. Early in the season, the wolves are still frequenting areas where humans congregate.

At the other end of the spectrum, if you do not see a moose during your visit, it is probably because you have cooped yourself up in a tent. Some years, there can be over a thousand moose on the island. In the summer, they tend to remain around Rock Harbor and Windigo. Smarter than they look, moose tend to hang around human settlements in the summer, while their predators avoid these areas. Moose prefer to feed in wetlands and at the edges of lakes. Occasionally, you may see one swimming across an inland lake, or even in Lake Superior.

There is a bounty of other wild animals on Isle Royale. Red foxes can steal their way into your camp and take your food if you are not careful. Bald eagles and loons frequent treetops and lakes. There are even garter snakes and painted turtles that somehow made their way across the frigid waters of Lake Superior.

It may be what is noticeably absent that really sets this place apart from all other places in the Upper Peninsula. The omnipresent coyote and white-tailed deer have not been seen on the island since the 1950s and 1930s, respectively. In fact, a hapless caribou was the last member of the deer family (apart from moose) to be seen on the island, in 1981! Rats, the scourge of biological diversity and common stowaways on boats, have not been seen in 80 years. In addition, the curse of the backpacker, the marauding black bear, is not present on the island.

America's largest island national park, Isle Royale is the premier opportunity for anyone wishing to experience wilderness in Michigan—this archipelago is isolated from the mainland. Minnesota is 17 miles away, and if you jump off from Michigan, you are looking at a 45-mile, five- to seven-hour boat ride.

You need to be prepared mentally and physically for backpacking on the island.

The nearest medical care can be three days away, rescues are done overland and by boat, and do not even think of bringing a cell phone—it is worth the same as carrying a rock in your pocket.

This pathway keeps you on the east end of the island, where there are more moose but fewer wolves. The footing is roots and rocks for nearly the entire way, so sturdy boots are in order. The weather is unpredictable: you can set foot on the island in dense fog and 45 degrees and, in less than an hour, lumber up to the Greenstone Ridge where it may be sunny and 90 degrees.

Upon arriving, check in at the ranger station and file your itinerary with park staff. This is your last contact with civilization for several days, so make sure all your equipment is present and in working order. As always, use Leave No Trace ethics. Nonburnable disposables are prohibited on the island, along with open fires.

ACCESS

Open from mid-April to mid-October, Isle Royale National Park is the only national park that closes for the winter.

From Houghton, take the six-hour *Ranger III* boat ride operated by the National Park Service. Copper Harbor is a little closer to the island, and the *Isle Royale Queen* can get you there in four and a half hours.

There are seaplane services to the island, operating out of Houghton, but the planes cannot fly in bad weather or fog. You can always take your own seaworthy boat across the lake. Rock Harbor can accommodate boats up to 65 feet long.

During its clockwise circumnavigation of the island, the *Voyageur II* provides drop-off and pickup service at several areas. Rock Harbor Lodge offers the M.V. *Sandy,* which provides a number of special tours. Also available out of Rock Harbor Lodge are a water taxi and motorboat and canoe rentals. Motorboat and canoe rentals are also available at Windigo. Travel on Isle Royale is on foot or by boat.

You must pay a $4 per person, per day *user fee* for each day you are on Isle Royale.

THE TRAIL

Day 1

Once you step onto the dock at Rock Harbor, your first order of business is to soak in the feeling that you are in a truly wild place. After coming to your sense of being, check in at the ranger station to plan and register your itinerary. Come with multiple plans, as the park limits the number of persons camping at each campground. For a little-used park, these designated campgrounds can become crowded places.

There is a maze of pathways in and around the ranger station and lodge, and several trails end at this point. You need to take the Tobin Harbor Trail, which is the second trail you will encounter (the first is Rock Harbor Trail) as you walk the paved path northeast from the ranger station. Take Tobin Harbor Trail, to the left (southwest).

You are immediately greeted by a clamber up a root- and rock-infested path. Get used to looking at the tops of your shoes for the next few days; this will be the primary scenery for much of your route.

Tobin Harbor Trail squeezes between Tobin and Rock Harbors for 2 miles, where a side excursion to Suzys Cave is found. If you choose to take the side trip, look for a cliff created by wave action, along with a sea arch. Both were formed when Lake Superior was at a higher level about 4,000 years ago.

Follow a bedrock ridge at the same relative elevation up to and past this point to the 3-mile mark, where another side trail on your south leads downhill to Rock Harbor Trail. Veer right and northward onto Mount Franklin Trail, cross Tobin Creek, then head up the bedrock face and look for piles of rocks, called cairns. These will be common trail markers on the trip. Remember, a cairn with a rock sitting on the right means stay to the right, and so on. Sometimes, you can lean a stick up on the pile pointing in the general direction.

Level out and climb up the famed Greenstone Ridge to an elevation of 1,000 feet, 400 feet above Lake Superior. Turning right will take you to a dead end on the southeast end of the island. Turning left will take you southwest towards Mt. Ojibway and farther on, Chickenbone Lake. Going straight will take you to Lane Cove Campground, little used by backpackers as it is on a dead-end trail, but popular with canoers. The isolation and nearness to the harbor (6.9 trail miles) make it a logical first camping destination. Cross the ridge and switchback your way onto the other side of the crest, losing most of your elevation, to Lane Cove, approximately 2.4 miles from the intersection.

Day 2

A typical morning at Lane Cove is spent waiting for the fog to burn off to enjoy the quiet, serene stillness of your wilderness setting. Loons are your alarm clock, and hunger is what motivates you to crawl out of bed, break camp, and eat breakfast, before retracing the 2.4 miles uphill back to the Greenstone Ridge. Take note that your only access to water today is at Lane Cove and Chickenbone Lake. Take in the irony: surrounded by the world's largest freshwater lake, you could actually run out of water today.

From the intersection to East Chickenbone Lake Campground, you will jaunt the remaining 8.5 miles along the backbone of the island. A few notable sights include Mt. Franklin, named after none other than Benjamin Franklin, about 0.3 mile from the intersection. You will stay right on top of the ridge, between 1,000 and 1,100 feet in elevation. You will roam through boreal forest and bedrock glades, and everything in between.

Mt. Ojibway tower (1,133 feet) is 2.7 miles farther along and is closed to climbing. Once used as a fire watchtower, today it houses scientific instrumentation that takes detailed climatological data. A junction to Daisy Farm and the Rock Harbor Trail heads south and downhill.

You are still on the ridge, but notice the beginning of a gradual decline. Although you will have many short ups and downs, the overall trend is downward. The Daisy Farm Trail comes in from your left in 1.5 miles from Mt. Ojibway, which just happens to be on an upward climb in elevation, back to 1,000 feet!

The remaining 4 miles is spent hugging the contour of the ridge, slightly downhill from the top as you approach Chickenbone Lake. When your course takes a hairpin turn and starts switchbacking downhill, you are about 0.2 mile from a trail intersection and 0.3 mile from East Chickenbone Lake Campground. Go straight at the intersection to the camp.

Day 3

Your second day was quite grueling, your feet are starting to hurt, and your legs are probably tired. Therefore, your third day will be rather short so you can quickly set up camp and spend some time fishing, exploring, or catching up on sleep.

Make a point to get up and pack out early to reach West Chickenbone Campground in time to choose your campsite. It sure beats groveling to share with already

A backcountry bay on Lake Superior

established campers, which is probably what you did last night.

March back uphill 0.1 mile to an intersection, turn right, and head southwest along the Greenstone Ridge Trail. A rather flat amble (by Isle Royale standards) is in order today as you trudge 1.8 miles to the intersection with the Indian Portage Trail. At the 0.9-mile mark, you will cross a stream and come close to Lake Livermore.

Turn right and head north on Indian Portage Trail toward West Chickenbone Campground, which is a downhill jaunt where you will lose about 100 feet in elevation from the Greenstone Ridge Trail.

Day 4

Your trip is halfway complete, and you will be heading back east toward Rock Harbor. With luck, you're well rested and recharged. Your next campground and today's final destination is Moskey Basin, 6 miles away on Lake Superior.

Stride back 0.1 mile using the Indian Portage Trail to the top of the ridge and cross over the Greenstone Ridge Trail. The first couple of miles will involve negotiating swamps, marshes, and some streams, as well as many bedrock and rooty climbs and descents. When a portage trail comes in from your left heading north to Lake LeSage, your course will flatten out in a marshy area then switchback down to Lake Richie and the campground at the 2.8-mile mark. At the 3-mile mark, head inland to another intersection, where you will head straight west, using Lake Richie Trail while the Indian Portage Trail will head south.

Climb 100 feet and level out (again by Isle Royal standards) and you can see a large marsh downhill on your right. At the 5.9-mile mark, descend in elevation, then take the spur trail to the campground.

Moskey Basin Campground is on a bay of Lake Superior. This is mostly a bedrock beach—no sand here. If you arrive early enough, occupy one of the screened-in, three-sided shelters. This campground is popular with canoers and is a great, open location to observe the night sky. You will be camping on a small, fingerlike projection on the bay, giving you a nearly 360-degree view, free of light pollution. Also, take time to listen as well, as there is no background noise from highways or other manmade activities.

Day 5

Today, you will learn a valuable lesson about backpacking on Isle Royale. If you surveyed every backpacker who has started their adventure at Rock Harbor, you'd find that well over half of them said they camped at Daisy Farm.

Your mission today is to avoid what seasoned Isle Royale backpackers call "crazy farm." Daisy Farm is very attractive, as it is 7.1 miles from Rock Harbor. Although Rock Harbor is closer (2.7 miles), this particular campground is at the intersection of two major trails and has plenty of space for hikers to camp.

Take your spur trail 0.1 mile back to your main route, which changes names to Rock Harbor Trail as you turn east. Climb up in elevation over the next 0.5 mile, and when you cross an unnamed intermittent stream, level out, noticing the Greenstone Ridge on your left and Lake Superior on your right.

Come to a gully holding Benson Creek, and switchback your way around and over the creek, descending 0.2 mile to lake level and Daisy Farm. You will see why it is so named: there is a large field full of wildflowers—including daisies, of course!

Rock Harbor Trail continues to parallel the edge of Rock Harbor. Although named after the body of water, it may have been appropriate to save some ink by leaving out the word "harbor." You will have fits, constantly scrabbling over large boulders and trying to avoid twisting your ankle. Because of all the obstacles, this segment can take you twice as long as you would normally expect.

Although the way may be rough, the views are unbelievable. Looking across the harbor, you'll see many islands sprouting out of the water, topped with evergreens. At 2.4 miles is Siskowit Mine, but it can be easy to miss. Your rock-infested route continues around Starvation Point at 3 miles, leaving 1 mile until Threemile Campground. Much quieter than Daisy Farm, it is heavily forested and there are some screened-in, three-sided shelters.

Day 6

Before breaking camp, check your departure schedule and budget your time accordingly. This could be a great day to sleep in, not having to rush to Rock Harbor to catch your transportation back to the mainland. On the other hand, you may want to get an early departure, hiking the 2.7 miles to take advantages of some services on the island you have done without for the past six days. There are showers at the ranger station, and even a restaurant at Rock Harbor Lodge.

At the 0.7-mile mark is a side trail to Suzys Cave, which is worth exploring. There is an abandoned mine at the 2.2-mile mark, but it can be hard to find due to the vegetation and rocks. Civilization, in the form of Rock Harbor and the ranger station, pop into view as you end your circuit of the northeast end of Isle Royale.

6

Lake Bailey Wildlife Sanctuary

Place: Lake Bailey Sanctuary

Total distance: 2 miles round trip

Hiking time: 2 hours

Gradient: Very difficult

High points: Unspoiled view of Lake Superior; plant diversity

Maps: USGS 7.5' Delaware

Amenities: None

Footwear: Backpacking boots

Pets: Prohibited

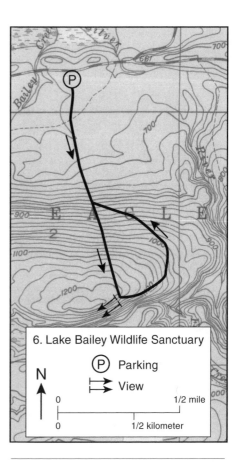

6. Lake Bailey Wildlife Sanctuary

(P) Parking

↦ View

N

0   1/2 mile

0   1/2 kilometer

SUMMARY

If you are looking for a climb and a great view, this is the place. However, pick your days wisely, as Lake Bailey Sanctuary is frequently fogged in. When you finally reach the top of this old mountain, hope for clear skies. The unspoiled views of the Keweenaw and Lake Superior are well worth the effort required to reach the top. More often than not, though, the summit will be blanketed in fog.

Mature cedars reach into the Keweenaw sky

Entirely wooded, Lake Bailey Sanctuary is a mix of cedar swamp in the low areas and northern hardwood forest during your climb. This Michigan Audubon wildlife sanctuary is known for its plant diversity, so bring a plant identification book.

The 2-mile round trip starts in a cedar swamp, which is usually dry enough to traverse in the summer. Look forward to the opportunity for a gut-wrenching climb to the top. The topography is steep; you will experience a 300-foot climb in less than 0.25

mile. The physical experience is worth it and rewarding. You are surrounded by more than 250 different species of plants, several of which are threatened or endangered. Look for the fringed polygala or rare heart-leaved Arnica.

This sanctuary has recently had an 80-acre addition, protecting the majestic trees that have mostly been free from lumbering. At the turn of the last century, only the largest of the trees were harvested from the area. Not surprisingly, the sanctuary is home to well over 100 species of birds.

ACCESS

From Eagle Harbor, take M 26 3.5 miles east. Parking area is just past the Lake Bailey public access.

THE TRAIL

Your day starts innocuously enough, wandering through a thick cedar swamp. Look around and think of the hard work that went into creating this treadway through the swamp. Although you're technically in a wetland, your footing is dry as you head into a cedar forest.

Walk out of the cedar swamp at 0.5 mile and you will be at the base of an ancient mountain that will make you feel old by the time you reach the top.

Rather steep, this will be a laborious trudge up 600 feet in elevation in about 0.5 mile. Catch your breath by taking breaks to identify the flowers and other plants sprouting through the thin soil. Ferns are rather plentiful as well, poking up under the canopy of northern hardwoods clinging on for dear life.

Although this is not a scramble, you will grasp small trees for balance, support, and for leaning up against to catch your breath.

At the summit is an amazing view south over the Keweenaw Peninsula. Catch your breath, take in the view, and feel gravity's pull as you descend using the return loop.

7

North Country Trail: Copper Peak to Mouth of Black River

Place: Ottawa National Forest

Total distance: 6 miles

Hiking time: 5–6 hours

Gradient: Moderately difficult

High points: Five waterfalls, rugged landscape

Maps: USGS 7.5' Black River Harbor, Copper Peak; NCT MI-14

Amenities: Semi-modern campground at Black River, harbor, picnic areas

Footwear: Backpacking boots

Pets: Not recommended

SUMMARY

Rugged and stunning, this short segment of the North Country Trail is Michigan's westernmost completed segment of this National Scenic Trail. The path is rock-strewn and rooty with several climbs and descents, so plan on taking longer than expected as this is far from a paved, flat footpath.

Starting at Copper Peak (worth checking out), the trail squeezes between Black River Road and the Black River.

Geologically, you will be witnessing rock formations from the Canadian Shield, which is billions of years old. Volcanic activity nearly 3.5 billion years ago created basaltic lava flows and metamorphosed sediments that were eventually uplifted and then eroded by various natural forces, including glaciers.

The Black River is only 30 miles long, but drops more than 1,000 feet in elevation as it journeys north to Lake Superior. Today, the river carries geologically young sediments as it slowly erodes the greenstones and granites that are billions of years old.

In these rocks were iron and copper, and it was none other than William Burt, General Land Office Surveyor and discoverer of Michigan's iron, who ventured here in 1847–1848 in search of copper. He discovered the Chippewa Mining Company, already well established and staking claims in the area. Various government agencies surveyed the area, but only small traces of copper were ever found.

This is a one-way trail, and since it will take you longer than you would expect, encourage one person in your entourage to meet you at the mouth of the Black River. The park is complete with a concession stand, a covered picnic pavilion, and even a marina. The North Country Trail crosses the Black River via a suspension bridge, and if your party wishes to see Rainbow Falls, they will have to grind up a torturous hill in order to reach them. Wave to them from across the river with a look of merriment, as you will have had a nearly level walk to the falls. However, do not let them know that.

If you are solo, camp at the Black River Recreation Area and use Black River Road to loop back to your parking spot, adding about 6 more miles to your travels.

After concluding your walk, take a ride to the top of the Copper Peak Flying Ski Hill. If you had done this at the beginning of your hike, and seen how far you had to walk, you probably would have quit right there on the spot. This astonishing view is best saved for the end of your hike. Copper Peak is synonymous with everything big. Rising more than 240 feet above the top of a 365-foot outcropping, this mammoth, cantilevered, 300-ton steel superstructure thrusts itself to an incredible 1,782 feet above sea level. One of Michigan's highest points, Copper Peak is almost 1,200 feet above Lake Superior.

For a priceless experience for a nominal fee, take the chair lift to the crest of the hill, and then take the 18-story elevator to an observation deck. If you have the guts, you can scramble up another eight stories to the summit for an uninterrupted view into Wisconsin and Minnesota. Notably, this is the least obstructed view in the Midwest. From the top, you can see more than 50 miles in every direction. Gazing for miles in every direction and seeing very few human impacts makes you realize that we truly live in an amazing state.

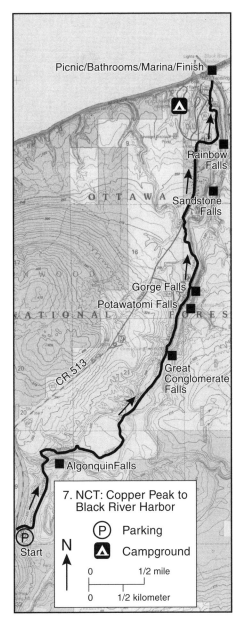

ACCESS

From Ironwood, drive west on US 2, turning north on Powderhorn Road (CR 513). The name changes to Black River Road 3 miles into your drive, after passing through

End your hike after crossing the Black River

Auvinen Corner. Continue on CR 513/Black River Road at almost 7 miles, making sure to veer right, following the signs for Copper Peak. The trailhead is on your right, 0.6 mile past Copper Peak.

THE TRAIL

At over a million square miles, the Ottawa National Forest is our westernmost, and also the largest, national forest in Michigan. With this much acreage, there are plenty of recreational opportunities. If you only have a day to spend, or need to get out of the car for several hours to stretch your legs, here is a three-in-one opportunity: a hike, a set of waterfalls, and the best unobstructed view in the Midwest.

If you need to get out of the car and away from everyone for a few hours, a one-way adventure is in order. The rest of your party can drive north on Black River Road to see the sights you will be passing.

Parallel the Black River, cradled in deep volcanic rock below grade. Do not even think of trying to take a sip of its golden-colored water—you would need technical climbing equipment to do so! The trail winds through the woods and will afford you several opportunities to view waterfalls along the way.

Head due east 0.2 mile through the hardwood forest of majestic hemlocks, massive white pines, and giant sugar maples to the edge of the river and start looking for your first waterfall, Algonquin Falls. These may be hard to see as you cut away, 1 mile into your trip, from the river just when you can hear the roar of the falls. There are social trails in the area that you could use, but be sure not to get lost!

The craggy volcanic rock underneath is tightly gripped by these trees, hanging onto existence in such a rough climate and environment. At the 1.1-mile mark, turn east, paralleling the river below. For the most part, you can hear but not see the river until it bends back to the north after another mile. You will be very close to the edge in places and you can definitely see the gash in the landscape cradling the Black River.

At the 3-mile mark, the Black River tumbles over Great Conglomerate Falls. Two more falls in rapid succession, Potawatomi at 3.5 miles, and Gorge Falls at 3.7 miles, are very popular with day users, as the parking area is visible from your current position. Boardwalks and overlooks that make for safe and easy viewing are present at these falls.

Continue to walk along the edge of the gorge holding the Black River, and at 4.5 miles, come out to Black River Road, where the hike becomes a road walk for 0.7 mile to get around some private inholdings.

Turn right at the drive for Rainbow Falls and head 0.2 mile back to the edge of the river. Rainbow Falls is visible from an overlook and, after soaking in the view, continue to head north. In 0.2 mile, head downhill into the harbor area, complete with a marina, picnic area, and bathrooms. Take the sidewalks toward the river's mouth and cross the footbridge and enjoy the geology.

8

West Shore–East Shore Trails (Presque Isle River Loop)

Place: Porcupine Mountains Wilderness State Park

Total distance: 2 miles

Hiking time: 2–3 hours

Gradient: Moderately difficult

High points: Waterfalls, geological formations, old-growth forest

Maps: USGS 7.5' Tiebel Creek; Porcupine Mountain State Park map

Amenities: Picnic area, pit toilets

Footwear: Hiking boots

Pets: Yes

SUMMARY

Aldo Leopold said it best when asked to express the call for saving the Porkies: "But the Porcupine necktie is more than timber; it is a symbol. It portrays a chapter in national history, which we should not be allowed to forget. When we abolish the last sample of the Great Uncut, we are, in a sense, burning books."

The Ojibwa called the area Kaugabissing, or "place of the porcupine," since the geological formations looked similar to the slope of a porcupine's back. Although you will not be penetrating into the depths of the Porkies, you will see a prime example of what Leopold was describing: uncut old-growth forest. At 65,000 acres, 25 miles long, 10 miles wide, and with 26 miles of Lake Superior shoreline, the entire park could take you weeks to explore.

The Presque Isle River Loop will give you a taste of the wild, rugged interior of the park without having to carry a week's worth of food on your back.

A popular walk for day hikers, the West Loop is part of the North Country Trail (NCT). Although the trail is short, this is rugged land with some dangerous components. It is very steep in places, and you will be walking right along the edge of the gorge with its 50-foot drops.

Three waterfalls—Manabezho, Manido, and Nawadaha—named after Ojibwa manitous, or "spirit warriors," are in full view from a series of boardwalks and observation platforms.

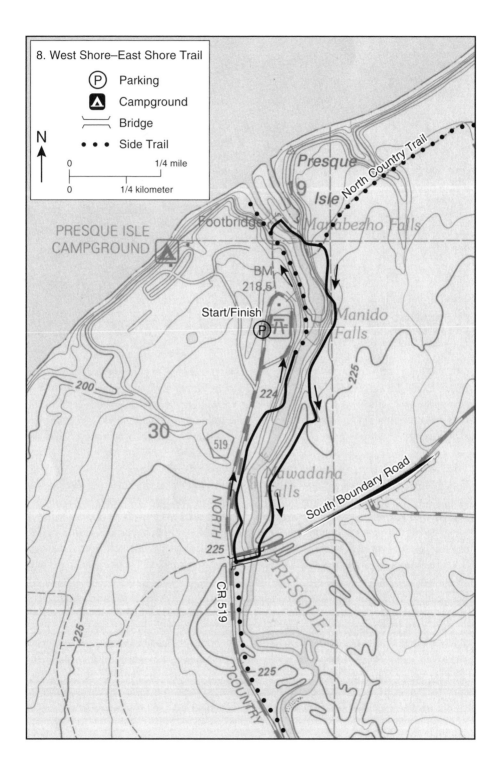

8. West Shore–East Shore Trail

Ⓟ Parking
🏕 Campground
⊐⊏ Bridge
• • • Side Trail

N

0 — 1/4 mile
0 — 1/4 kilometer

PRESQUE ISLE
CAMPGROUND

Presque
19
Isle

North Country Trail

Footbridge
Manabezho Falls

BM
218.5

Start/Finish
Ⓟ 🏕

Manido
Falls

225

200

30

224

519

Nawadaha
Falls

South Boundary Road

NORTH

225

CR 519

PRESQUE

225

COUNTRY

Nawadaha Falls

ACCESS
From Wakefield, go east on M 28 1 mile, turn north on CR 519, and drive 16 miles until the road ends at the Presque Isle River Unit. Park in the day use area.

THE TRAIL
Park in a heavily wooded parking area and then follow the well-beaten path to the north. When you reach the first intersection, turn toward the river's mouth, which is signed. The trail will split again in less than 0.1 mile, taking you either down a staircase or across a wooden footbridge. Note the NCT markers and take the footbridge across the gorge.

After crossing, immediately turn right, letting the NCT go straight into the woods. You will have the Presque Isle River on your right for your entire trek. Many social trails lead to the edge of the gorge, into the gorge, or down to the river. Probably your best opportunity to explore is immediately after crossing the footbridge and scrambling down to the volcanic formations, known as Nonesuch shale, cradling the Presque Isle River. Do this only during low water and when the rocks are dry, as slipping and sliding into a raging torrent likely would ruin your day.

It is amazing how such a short course can offer such great beauty—you'll be surrounded by old-growth white pine, hemlock, and yellow birch. It is also daunting to have some serious climbs to contend with as you are going upstream (uphill!) keeping pace with the elevation gains that create the three waterfalls. Be prepared for one particular climb that is a near scramble around the 0.5-mile mark of your excursion.

At 150 feet wide, the river valley carrying the Presque Isle could hold an enormous amount of water. The Presque Isle flows over Manabezho Falls on a rock shelf, descending 20 feet and causing the river to foam before its final journey to Lake Superior.

The prevalent geological formation, Nonesuch shale, was a primary indicator of copper deposits in the area. Geologists age this formation at just over one billion years.

Manido Falls is just 0.2 mile upstream, and the water descends over several rock steps, then some rapids, before flowing smoothly over shale.

Many day hikers abandon their walkabout at this point, not realizing that there is one more waterfall, Nawadaha. From your current position at 0.8 mile, you cannot see Nawadaha Falls from Manido Falls. You will have to negotiate a significant climb, almost a scramble, to reach the top of the gorge. Of course, this is what weeds out many walkers and prevents them from getting a nice, top-down view of the last of the three falls.

The shale is tipped slightly toward the east bank of the river, causing the Presque Isle to squeeze water over the Nawadaha Falls between the side of the gorge and the underlying shale. Be careful, as it is a 50-foot drop into the raging waters below.

As you approach South Boundary Road, descend slightly 0.1 mile before the road crossing. Climb up the embankment and use the bridge to cross to the other side. Be grateful that your journey back will be mostly downhill, and that the stretch between Manido and Manabezho Falls will be partly on boardwalks and level footing.

However, there is a significant decline near Nawadaha Falls that hugs the edge of the steep escarpment, and you will need to firmly grasp any small child's hand as you descend this sandy and rooty part of your quest.

Just before Manido Falls, there is a spur trail to your left that takes you to the parking area. Continue straight to complete the loop, turning left at a posted intersection to return to the parking area.

9

Oren Krumm Nature Trail

Place: Brockway Mountain Michigan Audubon Wildlife Sanctuary

Total distance: 0.7 mile

Hiking time: ½–¾ hour

Gradient: Moderate

High points: Overlooks, rare plants, migrating hawks

Maps: USGS 7.5' Lake Medora; Michigan Audubon trail map

Amenities: None

Footwear: Hiking boots

Pets: Prohibited

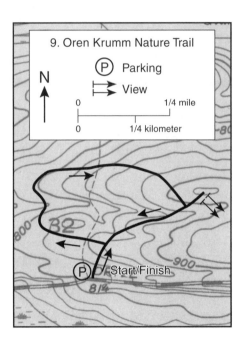

SUMMARY

This lollipop loop treats the hiker to different forest and successional stages, views of the Keweenaw Peninsula, and rock outcroppings. There are some steep inclines and loose footing in places. The stem of the trail can be muddy or even flooded after heavy rains.

The Michigan Audubon Society has protected this parcel to save several rare plants, including the heart-leaved Arnica. There are numerous plant species here, so bring along a plant identification book to thoroughly enjoy your experience. In the spring and fall months, migrating hawks fill the sky.

Prime's Pine or Pipsiwish

ACCESS

Take M 26 7 miles east from Eagle Harbor. Turn east on Brockway Mountain Drive, going 2.9 miles to the trailhead, which will be on the left, somewhat hidden due to the topography of the area.

THE TRAIL

The stem of the lollipop begins heavily vegetated and thick with grasses and ferns obscuring the path. In about 100 yards, enter a thick white cedar and white spruce forest, which is at a late pioneer stage. A bit higher in elevation, early pioneer trees like paper birch and poplar are starting to take hold.

At the intersection, which is not very noticeable, veer left in a clockwise motion. Climb up some rock outcroppings and look for a greenish tint. Exposed by glaciers when they receded 10,000 years ago, native copper is still present in many of the Keweenaw rock formations. Up on top of the ridge, you will veer west. A forest fire ripped through this area 90 years ago. Signs of this event still linger today. Look for what appears to be charcoal on the ground.

Heading west at 0.3 mile. Thin forest covers the top of the ridge, with loose footing underneath. The soil is thin and the climate is harsh, making it difficult for trees to take hold. It has been nearly one hundred years since the last major disturbance, and the forest is barely taking hold even now.

A spur trail at 0.4 mile to Lookout Point will give you another chance to scan for native copper, this time underfoot. On a clear day, you can see Lake Superior to the south. On a foggy day, which is much more likely, you will be lucky to see Brockway Mountain Drive a few tenths of a mile from your current location.

Bend back to the west, and head downhill again. Traversing an area where trees were blown down during a storm, you will be reunited with the stem trail. You will have that "Hey, I've been here" feeling about your stroll. Turning around, you will see the beginning of your trail splitting to the left.

Late spring is a great time to view migrating warblers. Other common residents include winter wrens, ruffed grouse, and least chipmunks.

10

Overlook Trail

Place: Porcupine Mountains Wilderness State Park

Total distance: 3.5 miles

Hiking time: 2–4 hours

Gradient: Moderate with some difficult stretches

High points: Old-growth forest, vistas

Maps: USGS 7.5' Government Peak; Porcupine Mountains Backcountry Guide

Amenities: None

Footwear: Backpacking boots

Pets: Not recommended

SUMMARY

The Overlook Trail is a loop, an offshoot connecting to the very popular Government Peak Trail.

You are entering a backcountry area complete with wild animals and wild views. The terrain is mostly uneven, and you will make a steep climb that will afford you some great views of the Porcupine Mountains, Lake Superior, and beyond into Minnesota if the weather is favorable.

This loop is used primarily by day hikers looking for a short but challenging walk. Because it leads nowhere, you should not encounter any backpackers.

You will experience two tales to the geology on your journey. The majority of your time will be spent climbing up the backside of a stratum known as Lake Shore traps, the fine-grained volcanic basalt that makes up the knobs and caps on most of the escarpments in the park. Take some time to examine some boulders and look for holes, which were created by gas bubbles when the rock was cooling. A good place to see Lake Shore traps is at the Lake of the Clouds Overlook.

Once you reach the summit, the rock formations at the overlooks are the reddish-brown Copper Harbor sandstone. This sedimentary rock has ripples created by water in the shallow seas that covered the area a billion years ago. If you are camping at Union Bay Campground, this sandstone makes up the beach on the Lake Superior shore.

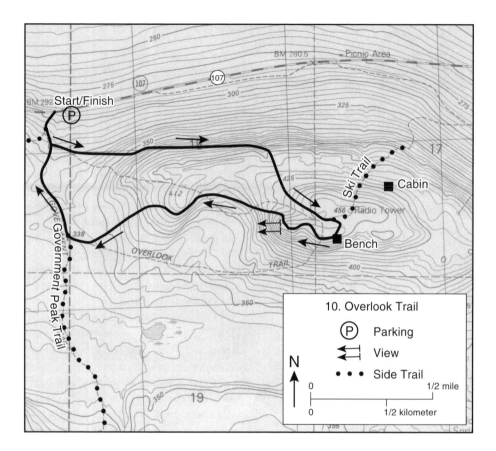

There are two overlooks, geological formations, and countless old-growth trees.

ACCESS

From Silver City, take M 107 into Porcupine Mountains Wilderness State Park. Pass the intersection of M 64, and the trailhead is 3 miles into the park on your left. The trailhead is marked Government Peak Trail. There is roadside parking.

THE TRAIL

Popular with backpackers, the Government Peak Trail is the gateway for hundreds of hikers every summer. You will stand out as a day hiker, not having to haul days' worth of supplies in a burdensome backpack. Instead, pack your ten essentials and head uphill on the wide, cobble-strewn path.

At 0.1 mile is an intersection with Escarpment Trail. Veer left, and 0.1 mile farther on, look for a sign on the right side of the trail. This is for the benefit of users leaving the Overlook Trail, directing them to the parking area and other nearby hiking trails. Turn left (east) into the forest.

About 100 yards from the intersection, quickly descend and climb out of a small valley holding the Cuyahoga River. After significant rains, this may be impassable, as

View to the west towards Lake Superior

there is no bridge. After climbing out of the valley, level out and follow the contour through maturing hardwood forest.

You are in a wilderness area, half sugar maple, half paper birch and balsam fir. Thimbleberry, red oak, and bigleaf aster carpet the forest floor. Blue metal diamonds lead you through the forest.

Your footing quickly trades the cobbles for roots and rocks. Turn inland from the creek, a slight incline. The blue metal diamonds continue; however, you will also see blue painted dots, more hemlocks, and even more thimbleberry.

Cross the contour of the mountain while slightly gaining elevation. Looking downhill, you'll have a view onto the tops of trees. Glancing uphill, you'll see many large boulders, some the size of small cars. At 0.5 mile from the intersection, keep following a more noticeable incline for 0.3 mile, slowly and gently climbing through mature hemlock and sugar maple.

Continue east, and when you turn south, you will just be a short distance from ramping up your adventure. Cross a rain-washed gully, then head southeast up a rib that parallels the gully. Exposed roots and rocks provide footholds and handholds, as you will be scrambling at times during this climb.

It is an anticlimactic, 200-foot climb to the top of the hill with no view other than the forest that surrounds you. Catch your breath as you even out and then change direction, heading mostly south. At the top of the mountain, the forest has lost most other species of trees, leaving it to the sugar maples. You must traverse a knob in the foreground—about a 30-foot elevation gain—and the open canopy on the other side indicates that you are about ready to summit, and enjoy a view.

Walk another 0.3 mile and at the 1.7-mile mark is the summit, where a ski track comes in from your left. Although you are at the high point, there is no view. After making a hard right to the west, surprisingly, there is no view, just a canopy of sugar maples. Take the track downhill, which is wide and well maintained. As you walk the edge of the heavily forested escarpment, an opening in the canopy finally welcomes you with a bench and a YOU ARE HERE sign that is for the benefit of skiers, not hikers.

Looking to the northwest, you can see the remnants of a four-billion-year-old mountain chain, the Porcupines. On a clear day, you can see a landmass in the distance: Minnesota.

Head inland, descend in and out of a small gully, and gently descend through mature hemlock and sugar maple forest. About 0.3 mile from the summit, notice an increase in the diversity of tree life including basswoods. Take a southward turn at 0.7 mile from the summit, while still encircled by mature old growth. Your footing becomes less rooty and rocky as you hike over the undulating landscape. The elevation drops off to the left, and you can see the sky through the forest canopy. Enjoy a second overlook, 0.6 mile from the previous one.

You will find evidence this is not a good place to hang out if there is an impending thunderstorm on the horizon. There are several large trees scarred by lightning strikes. A couple of trees look like they have exploded due to the force of the energy striking them.

The trail continues at a more moderate decline in a south-southwest direction. Turn more to the west 0.2 mile from the most recent overlook, and your footing becomes fairly flat. The forest takes on its normal composition of mature yellow birch, hemlock, and sugar maple.

The corridor continues to be wide and flat and intersects the cobble-strewn Government Peak Trail 0.2 mile later. Turn right and head downhill. You will pass your original intersection for the Overlook Trail 0.4 mile farther on, and then it is just a short 0.2 mile downhill to the parking area.

11

Summit Peak Trail

Place: Porcupine Mountains Wilderness State Park

Total distance: 1 mile round trip

Hiking time: 45 minutes

Gradient: Moderate

High points: Observation tower offers sweeping views

Maps: USGS 7.5' Underwood Hill

Amenities: Composting toilets, drinking water, interpretation station

Footwear: Tennis shoes

Pets: Yes

SUMMARY

Until 1958, Summit Peak (1,958 feet) was the highest point in Michigan. If you are puzzled, not having heard of a major geological event thrusting up and creating a new high point, do not fret. That year, two other peaks farther east near Baraga, Mt. Arvon and Mt. Curwood (elevations 1,978 and 1,979 feet, respectively) were discovered to be higher, relegating Summit Peak to third place.

This particular high point did not even have an official name recognized by the National Board of Geographic Names. It was known before 1956 as "the peak one mile south of Mirror Lake." Unromantic as that was, the name "State Summit" was suggested to recognize this as the highest point in Michigan. The name State Summit never stuck, but Summit Peak did. However, if you climb to the tops of Mt. Arvon and Mt. Curwood, there are no views whatsoever. Also, considering that you are higher than those two peaks when on top of the observation tower, it all is made up for!

Summit Peak, along with the Porcupines, were formed more than four billion years ago, when a mid-continental rift of volcanic action created a mountain chain that stretched from St. Louis to the Upper Peninsula, bending in a U shape south into the Lower Peninsula.

Summit Peak is made of the oldest rock found in the Porkies. This pinkish-gray igneous rock, called rhyolite, makes up most of the higher elevations in the park's interior.

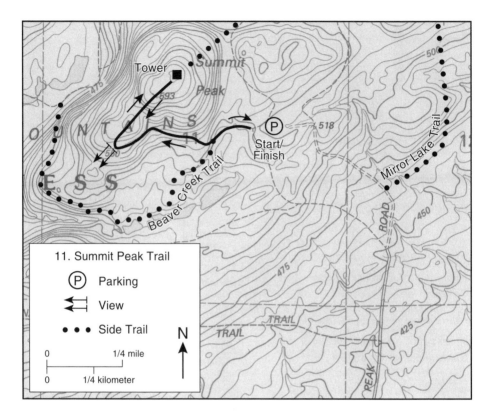

Numerous fault lines, mostly in the southeast part of the park, make for a great geology lesson. At the trailhead, there are interpretive panels that describe the geology in detail, including maps and photographs of the various volcanic rocks in the area.

The riskiest activity here is hiking during electrical storms. However, high winds accompanying these great storms have had a significant impact on the ecology of the area. Most notably, a strong storm on June 30, 1953 blew through the area with such great power and strength that it decimated about 5,000 acres of forest. The summit, with its height and exposure to the elements, was particularly hard hit. Old-growth trees, many several feet in diameter, were ripped out of the ground and scattered like tooth-picks. There is an overlook and a tower that takes you 30 feet above the peak. Enjoy a 270-degree view. On a clear day, you will be able to see Minnesota.

The Summit Peak Trail is popular with day users, as it is a relatively easy hike. Several benches and a boardwalk make the climb necessary to reach the tower somewhat easier. Although it is all uphill, the passage is wide and well maintained, and the crushed gravel trail surface makes for good footing. The trail is marked with blue painted dots for backpackers through-hiking the Beaver Creek Trail.

ACCESS

From Silver City, take M 107 west and turn south on South Boundary Road. Take South Boundary Road 12 miles to Summit Peak.

Vista from Summit Peak

THE TRAIL

This is a very popular area for day-trippers due to its shortness and the views it provides. Starting out, you will immediately encounter a sharp climb through the hardwood forest. Park planners saw the need for resting the weary, and there is a bench just 100 yards up the hill. The pathway continues to climb, crossing the contour of the hill, and there is another bench at the halfway mark, just when your course starts to level out and bend to your left.

An overlook to your left, down some steps to a deck complete with a telescope, welcomes those who need a break and a beautiful westward view, of the forests below and Lake Superior in the distance. This unspoiled vista reminds us of why the Porkies, and their continued preservation, are so important to us.

After enjoying the view from the overlook, turn around and head back up the stairs. An arch over a boardwalk indicates that Summit Peak is 0.3 mile uphill. The park has build a boardwalk that makes the walk easy on everyone—the alternative is ankle-twisting roots and rocks. It's a straight shot through the forest, but you will have to climb more than 100 steps spread out over this 0.3-mile walk.

The 30-foot observation tower sits at the top of Summit Peak, which is 1,958 feet above sea level. Let the wind blow through your hair as you collect your thoughts and admire the 270-degree view. On a clear day, you see nearly 100 miles into the distance.

To the northwest is Isle Royale National Park. Imagine standing on the edge of a large bowl. The depression that makes the bowl holds Lake Superior, and the edge on the other side is where the rock formation emerges again, only 50 miles away.

To the southeast is the smokestack from the White Pine Mine. This mine's heyday of harvesting copper was from 1955 until it shut down in 1995. Billions of tons of copper have been removed from the Precambrian Nonesuch shale, and the White Pine was the second most productive North American copper mine in 1964. A keen eye can see the massive pile of tailings—leftover rock waste from the mine.

Bergland Tower is just southeast of White Pine, and is one of the last remaining fire watchtowers in the Ottawa National Forest. Before the advent of airplanes and satellites, rangers with a penchant for soli-tude, elevated high above the tree canopy on the peaks of mountains and hills, would keep watch for forest fires.

Lake of the Clouds, although very close by, is obscured by a ridge covered in trees. Due north of your current position, you can make out the valley that holds this pristine lake.

An interpretive map at the tower and overlook identifies many of the features on the landscape. Take a camera, and your time, and enjoy one of the best unspoiled views in Michigan.

II

Iron Range

12

Tip Trail

Place: Point Abbaye Natural Area

Total distance: 0.8 mile round trip

Hiking time: ½ hour

Gradient: Flat

High points: Remote bedrock beach with extensive wave action

Maps: USGS 7.5' Skanee North

Amenities: Pit toilets

Footwear: Tennis shoes

Pets: Yes

SUMMARY

Point Abbaye is a minor peninsula to the east of the more dominant and better-known Keweenaw Peninsula. Remote and isolated, the road leading to this location is long and winding, but well worth the trip.

Flat, straight, and well used, Tip Trail brings you right out to the bedrock beach on Lake Superior. You are actually at the tip of the peninsula. Point Abbaye itself is just to the west.

ACCESS

Point Abbaye is 25.2 miles from the corner of Broad and Main Streets in L'Anse. Take Main Street north; its name eventually changes to Skanee Road. At 9.2 miles, turn north on Townline Road. At 13.8 miles, turn right on the gravel Point Abbaye Road. At 23 miles, the road reaches an unmarked Y-intersection in the road. Go left, and pass a private road called Macbeth at 23.8 miles. The road then becomes a narrow gravel two-track. Just 0.5 mile before the parking area, the thoroughfare becomes an even narrower, cobble two-track, then ends at the trailhead parking area.

THE TRAIL

Your adventurous drive to reach the parking area to access Point Abbaye will soon be worth it, as you take Tip Trail to the point. A large sign, with trails and mileages, sits adjacent to the trailhead. There are two other loops, Bay Trail and Woods Trail, however, they were not usable during this writing.

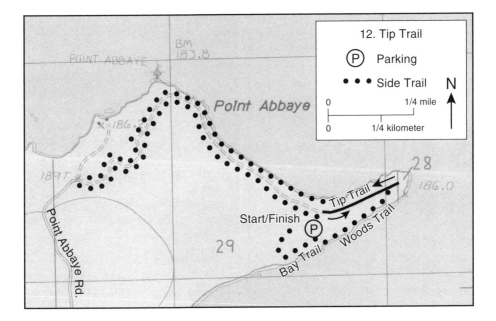

The Tip Trail is a cobble-strewn two-track that makes a straight shot for Lake Superior. Along the way, enjoy this walk through a typical northern hardwood forest that starts out dominated by paper birch accompanied by sugar maple and hemlock. Small balsam firs make up the shrubby ground cover, along with woodfern, starflower, Canada may-flower, large-leafed aster, and violets.

The trail is level, and the passage to the lake is straight. There are no markers guiding the way, though they are not needed. About 0.2 mile into your hike, take a slight bend to the left and you will notice some especially large cedars, red maples, and yellow birches.

The trail winds toward the point, and the forest becomes mostly dominated by sugar and red maples, with plenty of clubmoss covering the ground. Don't let a couple of social campsites at 0.3 mile and a social trail to your right to the east side of the point let you stray off course.

After leaving the woods, you will be abruptly greeted by the angst of Lake Superior, its waves crashing against the shore and hurling spray 10 to 20 feet into the air! You might feel as though you are in Maine, or at Big Sur in California, with the bedrock beach, large waves, and water collecting in the Great Lakes version of tidal pools, sans the starfish and anemones.

This is not a place to go swimming! Although the drop-off from the bedrock beach to the water may only be several feet in places at the point, the churning water and rip currents make this an unsafe place to take a dip. The actual point is rather small, about an acre in size. The rock formations and forest create a barrier preventing you from walking the beach. Instead, explore the volcanic rocks, some of which looks like freshly cooled magma. Large, moss-covered boulders balanced on the bedrock make for great photo opportunities and shelter you from the howling wind.

The bedrock comprising this beach may seem like a harsh environment. However, since the rock does not blow around or move the way soil or sand does, it makes for a great place for plants to anchor themselves to eke out an existence.

Crashing waves provide moisture and the dark rock absorbs sunlight, making this habitat more tolerable to plants than it might appear. Just as at Big Sur and along the Maine coast, there are three distinct "splash zones" that affect the plants that live here.

Closest to Lake Superior is the wave- and ice-swept portion of the bedrock. Very little plant life is found here. Further away is a zone dominated by lichens and mosses. Farthest from the shore is a zone dominated by low shrubs, including cinquefoils, dog-woods, and willows. You can find some soil development and even a few trees, like black spruce.

Yarrow, bearberry, marsh bellflower, pale painted cup, butterwort, dwarf primrose, and hairy goldenrod are all plants you could find on a bedrock beach.

Being out on the tip of a point, you can experience what biologists call the "penin-sula effect." As you move away from the mainland and toward the end of a peninsula, the number of species and the number of specimens of a particular species declines. Therefore, you probably will not see any large mammals like deer. However, there seems to be a healthy population of least chipmunks. These smaller relatives of the

Least chipmunk

very common eastern chipmunk have a dark stripe through the face, and the stripe on the back goes "at least" to the base of the tail.

Peninsulas, especially those with points such as Point Abbaye, can be funnels for birds crossing Lake Superior and heading south. They also can be launching points for flying organisms heading north in the spring. In late summer, keep your eyes open for migrating monarch butterflies making the trek over Lake Superior. In early fall, migrat-ing hawks and warblers may use Point Abbaye as a stopover.

In the springtime, birds such as blue jays may be jammed up and become rather nu-merous on a point such as this. Blue jays are not fond of crossing large bodies of water, so they tend to back up and create a bird's version of a traffic jam. So much for the peninsula effect!

13

Beaver Lodge Trail

Place: Bob Lake Campground, Ottawa National Forest

Total distance: 1.25 miles

Hiking time: 45 minutes

Gradient: Mostly easy, some moderate climbs and descents

High points: Beaver dam, old railroad grade, interpretive trail

Maps: USGS 7.5' Rousseau

Amenities: Rustic campground with swimming beach

Footwear: Hiking boots

Pets: Not recommended

SUMMARY

Beaver Lodge Trail, an interpretive trail with a brochure handout for your learning pleasure, takes you along an old logging railroad grade and into a hardwood forest. Making a lollipop loop, you will have an easy passage here with the exception of a couple of moderate staircases to negotiate.

Bob Lake is situated in a fairly remote part of the Ottawa National Forest. Far from the beaten path, you will likely have the woods all to yourself.

Beaver Lodge Trail winds into the woods as it makes the loop. Constructed in 1968 by the Ojibwa Civilian Conservation Center in cooperation with the Office of Economic Opportunity, the area has held up very well and is clearly marked with the name of the trail, using a beaver as its logo.

ACCESS

From M 28, take FH 16 north 12 miles, and turn left on Pori Road. Take Pori Road 2 miles and turn left onto USFS 1470. Go 2 miles, and turn left onto Bob Lake Road. Follow the road into campground, all the way to the end. Parking and trailhead are adjacent to the pit toilet.

THE TRAIL

Begin by winding through a young maturing forest with a diverse mix of balsam fir, large-tooth aspen, ground cover with sarsaparilla, and mosses. You reach your first interpretive sign telling you the story of all the uses for paper birch. Most people know that

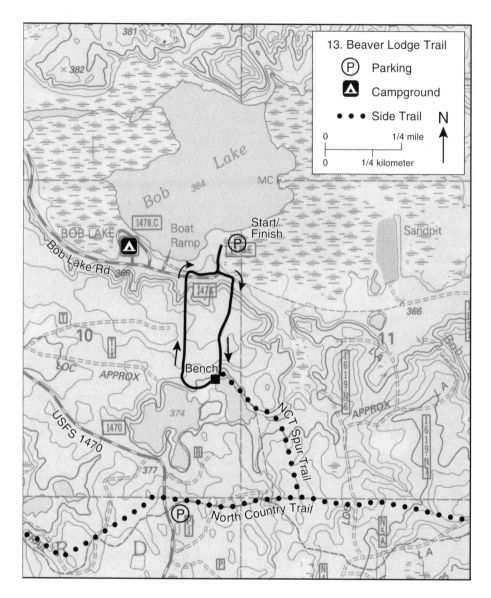

13. Beaver Lodge Trail

P Parking

▲ Campground

• • • Side Trail

N

0   1/4 mile

0   1/4 kilometer

paper birch bark was used to make great canoes. Today, shed paper birch bark makes good kindling for starting fires due to the abundance of oil in its fibers.

The second interpretive sign tells you about the floating bog to your right, which explains why the lay of the land is so flat in this stretch. Tamaracks and black spruces sprout from the floating sedge mat when it becomes thick enough to support the weight of these trees. Take a close look at a tamarack. Is the trunk slightly crooked in places? This is because, as the tree settles to one side, the trunk adjusts by growing straight. Every time it moves, a crook forms as the tree tries to right itself.

On the Beaver Lodge Trail

Pass the sign about aspen (or popple), and the ground cover reveals false Solomon's seal before you reach the next sign, identifying a nonexistent burl that probably used to be found here at one time. Burls are a tree's reaction to a foreign substance or a reaction to an injury, as humans create scabs and then scars when our tissues are disturbed.

What appears to be a woodshop project on your right is an interesting guide to identifying trees. Line up the viewfinder with a nearby tree and it will name it for you.

At 0.2 mile, come to an intersection with the return loop, identifying the trail and its connection to the nearby North Country Trail.

This segment of trail was created in the late 1800s, and some of the original ties remain and can be seen later. The original old-growth forests were completely logged over at the turn of the 20th century. Nearby, the Red or Gallagher Camp was 0.25 mile to

the east of your current location. The grade came to the lake, to access the water for use at the camp. Cross the road and take a moderately steep staircase up about 30 feet to the top of a plateau in the hardwood forest.

Cross the contour of the hill, noticing the drop in elevation to your left and the top of the hill to your right. At the top there is a bench, and you are surrounded by maturing hardwood forest, mostly sugar maple with some woodfern and small sugar maples making up the ground cover.

Level out and your next graphic identifies an uncommon tree in this forest—basswood. Basswood is a popular wood for carving and prefers moist to slightly wet soils. You would expect this tree with its heart-shaped leaves to be growing along the edge of the swamp below. Peel away from the drop-off and progress in the general direction of the campground. Reach a small, pothole wetland with another interpretive panel identifying an old white pine stump that was cut in the late 1800s and yielded more than 2,600 board feet of lumber!

Pass the pothole and you'll see a graphic telling the story of how small wetlands like these are formed, and their importance. Filled with sedges, it probably holds water only in the late winter and early spring.

Bend to your right, taking the general direction back to the campground as the trail rolls over the landscape and to the next sign, for sugar maple.

The trail descends across the contour, taking you downhill to the edge of a wetland, and at 0.8 mile, the spur to the North Country Trail. There is a very prominent STOP sign, preventing day hikers from taking this trail, as it does not lead back to the parking lot, but to New York or North Dakota.

The wetland is a massive beaver pond, with several interpretive graphics with information about beavers, the creation of this wetland, and other wildlife that benefits from beavers. Several plank boardwalks keep your feet dry as you negotiate between the beaver pond, the nearby wetlands, and the forest. What appears to be a lengthy grass-covered hill between you and the pond is the remnants of beaver lodges built over time.

Come to a bench, and a sign telling the story of two young beavers that tried to set up a home in this area. Make a hard right and go uphill back into the woods past a botanical lesson on the bracken fern and the work of the pileated woodpecker.

The terrain levels out and undulates, and the trail enters a stand of mature hemlock, which is a winter shelter for animals like deer. Slowly decline, and follow a gully on your left. Look into the distance and you can see the forest road about 300 yards straight ahead.

The work of a yellow-bellied sapsucker is evident in a hemlock tree and identified by another panel graphic. At 1 mile, continue downhill with the ravine on your left, descend a staircase, cross the gravel road, and come back to the old railroad grade. Turn right, and continue to follow the interpretive graphics telling the story about the logging camps, railroad grade, and sphagnum moss growing in the remnants of the swamp on your left. Looking closely, you'll see that black spruce, black ash, red maple, tamarack, balsam fir, and cinnamon fern are resident here.

Your final graphic thanks you for taking the time to visit the Beaver Loop Trail today. Turn left at the next intersection and head back to the parking area.

14

Bog Walk and Nature Trail

Place: Presque Isle Park

Total distance: 0.3 mile

Hiking time: ½ hour

Gradient: Easy

Highpoints: Bog, beach

Maps: USGS 7.5' Marquette

Amenities: Presque Isle Park, beyond having picnic areas and bathrooms, also has a marina and a swimming pool.

Footwear: Flip-flops

Pets: Yes

SUMMARY

Marquette is probably Michigan's best example of a "trail town." Skiing, hiking, and mountain biking are very popular activities in the city that hosts Northern Michigan University. Most of Marquette is mountainous and rugged, and there are plenty of paths for skiers and bikers to choose from.

It is very difficult to find one trail that best exemplifies Marquette. The Bog Walk and Nature Trail is highlighted here because it is not a rough trail, and bikes and skiing are not allowed here. As a hiker, you will have a nice quiet walk without worrying about getting out of the way for a trail user on a bike.

Located at the entrance of Presque Isle Park, this nature trail was built and paid for by the Marquette Rotary Club in 1986. This club still takes the time and resources to maintain this trail over 20 years later. This 323-acre park has a full slate of amenities, from pavilions, a band shell, and gazebos to playgrounds and even a swimming pool. These facilities are concentrated at the entrance of the park, adjacent to your trail.

The bog is estimated to be 10,000 years old and has survived many human activities over time, especially in the last 200 years. Docks and boardwalks give you an intimate look at the plant life growing in a habitat most people never venture into.

ACCESS

From downtown Marquette, drive north on Fourth Street, which changes into Presque Isle Avenue. Turn right (east) onto Hawley Street and continue to Lakeshore Boulevard.

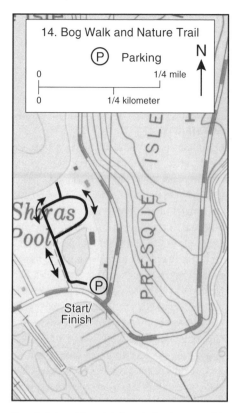

14. Bog Walk and Nature Trail

(P) Parking   N

0 ——————————— 1/4 mile

0 ——————————— 1/4 kilometer

Sh*ras Pool*

Start/Finish

Turn left (north) and follow Lakeshore until it ends at the park entrance. Instead of passing through the entrance, look to the left, across from the marina, for the trailhead and a gravel parking lot.

THE TRAIL

In the shadow of a coal-fired power plant and a dock for ocean freighters hauling iron ore, the Bog and Beach Trail can help you escape from knowing there is such heavy industry so close by. Right next door is a swimming pool, and there's a marina across the street.

This is a lollipop loop with two turnouts and a couple of trails allowing access to Lake Superior. Tread on asphalt through a field, which in the late summer sports many blooming tansy plants.

The interpretives mostly tell the story of the natural history of the area. The first sign points out that this bog has been filled in over time and only a small remnant remains. In the meantime, many invasive plants, including bull thistle, burdock, Queen Anne's lace, and raspberries, have come into the area and are apparent in the open field in front of you.

Leave the asphalt and walk onto a wooden boardwalk and you will come to your first spur, on your left, which brings you into the heart of the small bog. The dominant shrub is leatherleaf, a bog staple. This low, evergreen shrub grows in large clumps on top of sphagnum moss. Leatherleaf is a great shrub for nesting birds, as it protects them from marauding predators. Because of the leatherleaf, there is more bird activity here than in the surrounding landscape.

Leave the spur, turn left, and skirt the edge of the bog through a mowed grassy area. Come to your second elevated boardwalk on the left and take that into the bog.

Leave the spur, turn left again, and approach a bench and a large mowed opening. Veer left onto another boardwalk that takes you across what the trailhead map calls a pond, but which definitely still has its bog character. Sweetgale grows very thick in the bog. This low shrub's parts are pleasantly fragrant when crushed. Sweetgale was formerly used in clothing to repel moths, and Native Americans are thought to have dyed porcupine quills with this plant.

Keep your eyes and ears open for white-throated sparrows, catbirds, and even brown thrashers.

A total transition between habitats takes place as your bog boardwalk ends and you find yourself on the backside of a small sand ridge adjacent to Lake Superior. Turn right and note several side trails to your left that gain you access to the beach. The sand

A spur trail takes you to a bay on Lake Superior

ridge has beach grass, and Lombardy poplars–probably planted to stabilize the area–are growing on the top of the ridge. The bog is on your right as you walk the backside of this sandy ridge.

Bend back inland on a mowed path, and the bog is still on your right. Straight ahead, you can see the swimming pool and water slide. Circumnavigating the bog, you will cut through a small grove of trees and come back to the bench in the large mowed area, completing your lollipop loop.

Consider driving in Presque Isle Park, as there are more trails in the park, as well as several spur trails that give you great views of the harbor, Lake Superior, and Marquette.

15

Cascade Falls Trail

Place: Cascade Falls, Ottawa National Forest

Total distance: 1.6 miles

Hiking time: 1–1½ hours

Gradient: Valley Trail is easy; Bluff Trail has very difficult climbs and descents.

High points: Views of trap hills, waterfall

Maps: USGS 7.5' Matchwood NW

Amenities: None

Footwear: Hiking boots

Pets: Not recommended

SUMMARY

This is a tale of two very different trails that can accommodate both serious trekkers and casual hikers who like to keep sweat to a minimum. First, take the lower, easier trail downhill to the waterfall.

After thoroughly exploring the waterfall, take the spur trail back to the intersection of the lower trail and the upper trail. Those short on time and weak of spirit (and knees) can just double back on the trail whence they came. Those who are more adventurous and looking for great views can turn up the upper trail and start climbing. This is a great quest if you don't have time to fully experience the North Country Trail weaving through the Trapp Hills, as you'll be given a taste with a couple of superb views.

ACCESS

From Bergland, take M 28 East 2 miles, and turn north on FR 400. This is a one-lane gravel road with turnouts. The road to Cascade Falls is 6 miles north of M 28. After crossing Cascade Creek on a one-lane bridge, turn right and the parking area is 0.3 mile into the woods.

THE TRAIL

Immediately, you are tempted to take the trail to the left. Take a gander: it is a steep, rocky climb, as evidenced by the protruding volcanic rocks. Instead, continue on the well-worn main lower trail marked with blue plastic diamonds. As is typical of the western Upper Peninsula, you will mostly be in northern hardwood forests dominated by

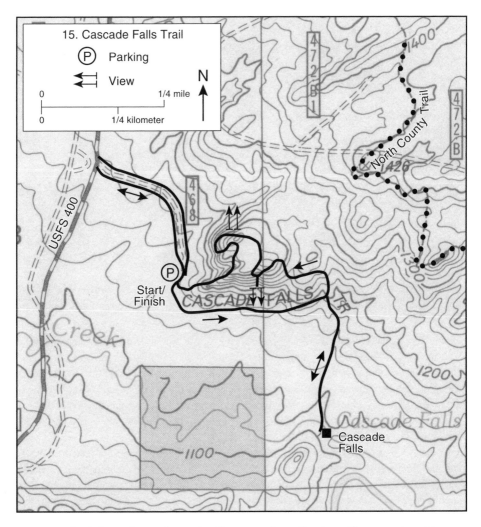

P Parking

View

N

0   1/4 mile

0   1/4 kilometer

472 B 1

North County Trail

472 B

426

1400

4 6 8

USFS 400

Start/
Finish

CASCADE FALLS TR.

Creek

1200

1100

Cascade Falls

Cascade
Falls

sugar maple, balsam fir, poplar, and white spruce. Ground cover consists of starflower, large-leaf aster, bracken fern, and small, emergent maples popping up through the roots and rocks covering the ground.

Descend slightly through the forest. The soil will then begin to ripple slightly as you head toward the waterfall. At 0.4 mile, you will reach the second intersection between the two trails. Take a look; it is a steep climb up. If the first time convinced you to labor up it (or not hike at all!), the second inter-

section will only reaffirm your thoughts.

Turn left and progress downhill on a gentle slope. Just 0.1 mile from the trail intersection, cross a small gully on a footbridge. The habitat becomes more mesic in structure, and you'll walk by basswood, red oak, black ash, speckled alder, more balsam fir, and fewer sugar maples as you go downhill. The trail is probably sticky in wet years, due to the swampy feel of the forest. On my last visit, it was very dry and the ground had giant cracks from desiccation, looking like a

Cascade Falls

dried lake in some Western desert.

With the decline, the vegetation becomes thicker, although it does lose the overhead canopy. Beware of a thick patch of poison ivy in a short stretch of trail. Sedges camouflage this irritating plant, so know your "leaves of three, let it be" mantra.

About 100 yards from the river, white pine and hemlock sprout from the shore of Cascade Creek. The gash on the landscape caused by this small tributary of the Ontonagon River exposes the volcanic rocks that create the falls.

The falls has two cascades, and it is easy to maneuver and even cross the river during low water. Upstream, it appears canoeable, even during times of drought. Gaze downstream, however, and the rocks will deter even the bravest of kayakers from venturing forth.

After fulfilling your fix for waterfalls, head back to the intersection of the two trails. Part ways with those less brave, and head uphill. Less used than the lower, main trail,

the upper trail is a thin track marked with blue plastic diamonds. Level out, turn, and follows the contour for 0.2 mile. Climb slightly and you will see a rock outcropping on your right. Turn right and experience a moderate climb uphill over rooty and rocky footing.

On your left, notice a volcanic knob sprouting out of what resembles a mesa, upon which you are walking. It appears that you are walking around the knob when the trail suddenly vaults upward, using a switchback, to get you to the top of the knob. Your jaunt becomes moderately difficult, just short of scrambling; you are climbing about 50 feet in elevation in a very short stretch of trail.

At the summit is your first view of the wide expanse making up the Ottawa National Forest to the south. The vegetation is thin and the trees are scrappy, trying to make a living on a thin smattering of soil on this volcanic outcropping. Notice a pioneer species, staghorn sumac, thriving at the top of the hill.

Follow the edge of the escarpment, checking out more views of the valley below. Skirt into the woods for a couple hundred yards while noticing that paper birch and sugar maple make up the majority of the trees here. Make a moderate descent taking you to the north side of the mesa, with another escarpment and another knob. Climb 20 feet in about 100 feet of walking up to another view to the west.

It is hard to believe that this entire are was completely logged off at the turn of the last century. With one hundred years of growth, you would never guess that this area was decimated and devoid of trees at one time.

Today, the forest is healthy and although there is logging in some areas, you cannot see any signs of this activity here.

Keep following the escarpment and you will start losing elevation, and continue to have views to the west, including a basalt outcropping and cliff face in the distance. Continue your moderate descent with some steeper portions. When the ground is wet, your footing will be a slippery mess, so this trail is probably best left for when it dries up.

The trail ends with a steep decline and immediately levels out at the trail intersection, a mere 100 feet from the trailhead.

16

Cedar River and Ridgewood Trail

Place: Wells State Park

Total distance: 2.2 miles

Hiking time: 1–2 hours

Gradient: Easy

High points: Natural sand beach, Civilian Conservation Corps (CCC) history

Maps: USGS 7.5' Cedar River; Wells State Park map

Amenities: This is a modern state park, however, the nearest towns with services are Menominee (25 miles south) and Escanaba (28 miles north).

Footwear: Tennis shoes

Pets: Yes

SUMMARY

Wells State Park was donated to the State of Michigan in 1924 by the children of John Walters Wells, a lumber baron, as a tribute to an unusual action he took in the late 1800s. Wells was responsible for saving an 800-acre parcel of forest containing uncut pine, beech, hemlock, and spruce—the very trees that had made him a rich man.

The park has 3 miles of beach along Green Bay, most of which is in its natural state. Although you'll be in full view of the natural beach, you will be entirely within mature forest. This is a level walk, passing by a few structures built by the CCC in the 1930s and 1940s.

ACCESS

From Escanaba, take M 35 south for 28 miles. After passing the Cedar River, Wells State Park is on the left in 1.5 miles. Park at the day use area.

THE TRAIL

Walk back up the entry drive to the day use area, and turn left into the campground. Follow the loop closest to the lake. The trail enters the woods at campsite #50 and at a trail shelter built by the CCC. Although missing its roof, it is still functional with benches and a fireplace.

The passageway is wide and flat, making its way through a mature hemlock, white pine, and cedar forest. To your right, down a 10-foot embankment, is the cobble beach covered in native grasses, flowers, and

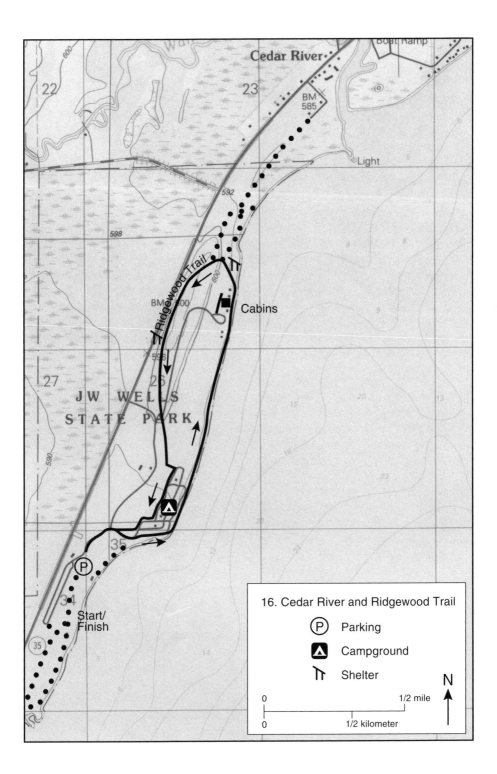

Cedar River

22
23
BM 585
Light
592
598
Ridgewood Trail
BMgewood 700
Cabins
27
26
JW WELLS
STATE PARK
550
35
P
34
Start/
Finish
35

16. Cedar River and Ridgewood Trail

(P) Parking

⛺ Campground

⛺ Shelter

N

0   1/2 mile
0   1/2 kilometer

A Civilian Conservation Corps trail shelter

shrubs. There are numerous social side trails, and at any time you can access the lake to see what a natural beach looks like.

Being along the lakeshore, this is a great place for witnessing bird migrations. In late May and late August, migrating warblers flit about in the vegetation. If you are into the general enjoyment of these birds without the worry of strictly identifying each species, either season will suffice. Stick to the spring if you are into identification, unless you are well versed in what many birders call "confusing fall warblers," which look nearly identical from one species to the next.

Wild sarsaparilla carpets the ground in many places. This ginseng relative has an umbrella-like leaf divided into three groups of five leaflets each. Flowers are green and take on a "popcorn ball" appearance at the end of a naked stalk. Look for deep purple, almost black, berries in the late summer and fall. The berries and roots were once used to make root beer.

Marked with Michigan Department of Natural Resources (DNR) pathway trail markers, your trail is mostly dry, however, you'll need to pass thorough a low, swampy area, which will be on your right. Look for exposed drainage pipes on the ground.

Take this opportunity to explore the natural sandy beach, as you will soon turn inland. Sand beaches on the west side of Lake Michigan are spared the scraping and trauma caused by winter ice that the beaches on the Lower Peninsula see. Native phragmites, cinquefoils, dogwoods, native swamp rose, willows, and bulrushes can crowd the beach, making it difficult for you to make it to the water.

Many herring and ring-billed gulls, shorebirds, and waterfowl are attracted to the natural sand beach. The lakeshore is used as a migration corridor for birds headed south for the winter or north for the summer. Be prepared for fog, as a prevailing westerly wind with moister, warmer air frequently condenses over the lake, creating a murky setting.

At 0.7 mile, you'll reach six cabins that are available for rent. The habitat is mostly open here, with hand pumps and pit toilets for the cabin users. Reenter the mature forest 0.1 mile beyond the rental cabins to see another trail shelter made by the CCC. This one still has its roof. Begin to peel away from the lake about 0.1 mile past the shelter, and you will come to a signed intersection. Turn left onto the Evergreen Trail to return to the parking area for the rustic cabins. Continue straight on the Cedar River Trail 0.1 mile until the next intersection. Turning right brings you back to the campground using the Ridgewood Trail. Continuing straight will bring you to Cedar River Harbor.

Climb a small hill and parallel M 35, listening to the roar of the highway. At the top of the hill, through the trees, you can see vehicles hurtling to their unknown destinations. Don't let the howl of traffic get you down—there is plenty of hiking left and plenty to see.

You can play a woodland scavenger hunt; keep your eyes open for ostrich fern, American beech, maidenhair fern, and pileated woodpecker holes. Turn away from the highway back into the woods slightly, and 0.3 mile from the start of the Ridgewood Trail, to a third trail shelter, similar in construction to the other two. Look for roosting bats in the rafters during daylight hours. The woods become very open, with little or no shrub layer. Sarsaparilla dominates the forest floor. In a good year, there would be enough material to make gallons of root beer!

At 0.6 mile, cross the gravel road leading to the cabins, snake through some young forest, and you will come to a trail intersection. To the right is the park's contact station. Turn left, and you will come out of the woods at campsite #121. Turn right and follow this loop until it leaves the campground.

17

Clark Lake Trail

Place: Sylvania Wilderness

Total distance: 8.2 miles

Hiking time: 5–6 hours

Gradient: Moderate

High points: Pristine wilderness lake setting, great fishing, old-growth forests

Maps: USGS 7.5' Black Oak Lake; Ottawa NF Sylvania Wilderness Map

Amenities: Bathrooms, picnic area at trailhead

Footwear: Backpacking boots

Pets: Not recommended

SUMMARY

Some call it "Michigan's boundary waters." Remote, pristine, and wild sums up the sights around Clark Lake, part of the Sylvania Wilderness in the Ottawa National Forest. Although Sylvania attracts mainly canoers, a small number of campers, backpackers, and hikers are called to its expansive virgin forests.

Backpacker magazine considers this trek one of the best in the Upper Midwest. Therefore, the good news is that the trail is well used. The bad news, since this is a wilderness area, is that there are no markers or posts directing your way. A good rule of thumb is to keep Clark Lake on your right (if walking clockwise), and of course, carry a map and compass.

It is difficult to get lost here, but you can get lost in your thoughts, marveling at the massive white pines. These are the closest objects resembling skyscrapers, and, at over 100 feet tall and hundreds of years old, they have endured longer than most.

When you have old trees, you will have old roots protruding from the ground. If you are at all familiar with the Iron Range, you know that this is part of the deal. In addition, billion-year-old chunks of rock are scattered about.

More than 35 spring-fed lakes nestled between the Mississippi and Great Lakes watersheds ensure a quality outdoor experience in the Sylvania Wilderness. You can make this into an overnight adventure or even a two- or three-day backpacking trip, as there are five campgrounds along this

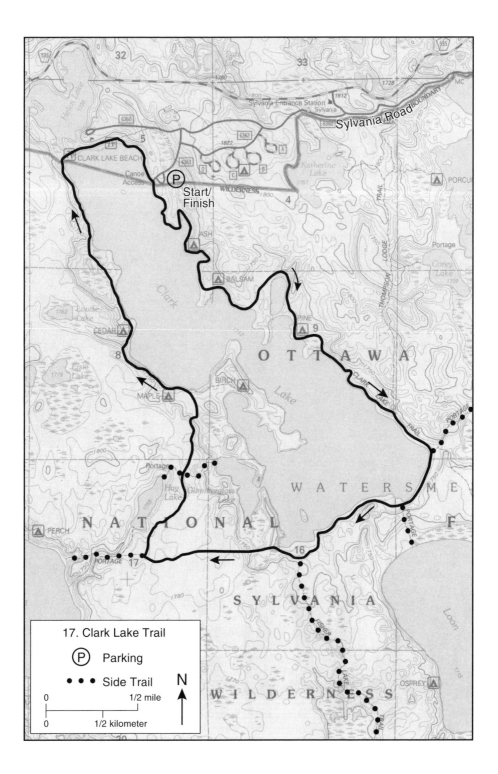

32   33

Sylvania Entrance Station
Sylvania

Sylvania Road

MC

Helen Lake

6360

5

CLARK LAKE BEACH

Canoe
Access

P

Start/
Finish

1822

6362

6361

Q

C

B

A

Katherine
Lake

PORCU

WILDERNESS

4

THOMPSON LODGE

Portage

Corey
Lake
1709

ASH

BALSAM

PINE 9

Clark

Louise
Lake
1782

CEDAR

8

Elsie
Lake
1779

MAPLE

O T T A W A

Lake

CLARK LAKE TRAIL

PORTAGE

BIRCH

Portage
Hay
Lake

Gimmerglass
Lake

W A T E R S M E

PORTAGE

F

PERCH

N A T I O N A L

PORTAGE 17

16

Loon

S Y L V A N I A

1780

FISHER

1770

OSPREY

W I L D E R N E S S

17. Clark Lake Trail

Ⓟ   Parking

• • •   Side Trail

N

0   1/2 mile

0   1/2 kilometer

hike. Visitors especially like the south end of Clark Lake, where at least 80 acres of white and red pine have survived the axe—one of Michigan's few remaining patches of old-growth forest.

Wildlife abounds, clinging to life around the lakes, six of which are larger than 250 acres. River otters, black bears, wolves, ospreys, and eagles roam the forests, keeping a wary eye on human intruders.

Proximate to a day use area and campground, pitch your tent, then venture south into the wilderness area for an easy day trip. Take a canoe and you can lose yourself for a week, exploring all those crystal clear lakes.

If canoeing is not your thing, you can backpack around many of the lakes, using portages and shorelines. There are plenty of designated campsites under towering white pines. Fishing is popular, but special rules apply, so you will need to enquire when registering. Bring your binoculars to view the abundant birds, including bald eagles, loons, and the curious gray jays.

ACCESS

Sylvania Wilderness is easily accessed off US 2, just west of Watersmeet. Take Thousand Island Road about 7 miles until you reach the parking area at the north end of Clark Lake. There is a campground adjacent to the lake. The trailhead starts at the south end of the canoe access parking area.

If you plan to spend the night in the wilderness area, you will need to get a permit and attend an orientation program before embarking. Motorized boats are allowed only on two lakes (Crooked and Long) in the Sylvania Wilderness, so you will have a quiet experience.

Camping is permitted at designated sites by permit only. Permits can be acquired on a walk-in basis at the Sylvania Wilderness entrance station or can be reserved through

Reserve America at www.reserveamerica.com or 1-877-444-6777.

Day hikers to Sylvania will be charged a day use fee between May 15 and September 30 annually. Day passes are $5, wilderness campsites cost $10 per night, and the fee is $12 per night to camp at the Clark Lake Campground.

THE TRAIL

Before you enter the wilderness, you will be asked to wipe your feet.

Although your cleats may pick up and become clogged with Sylvania's soil, the exercise here is to remove any stowaways before entering the forest—the primary threat is garlic mustard, the scourge of many forests in Michigan's Lower Peninsula. Although you may have yet to see garlic mustard rear its ugly head in any part of the UP as of yet, the Ottawa National Forest is being proactive in preventing the spread of this and other nasty plants. So wipe your feet!

The well-used, wide, unmarked trail takes you along the edge of Clark Lake for about three quarters of your escapade. Several portages cross and intersect the Clark Lake Trail, so pay particular attention to your whereabouts. You should not have to be reminded to carry a map and compass on this hike. Your chances of needing them are much greater here than on other hikes described in this guide.

Feel free to take a social trail to the lake's edge to admire the scenery, wildlife, or a friendly canoer gliding across the clear water. You will hug the shore quite tightly, bending around every bay and cove.

The habitat is mostly old-growth white pine, hemlock, and yellow birch. The ground cover is sparse, since so little sunlight makes it through the thick and mature canopy. Although rooty and rocky, there are fair stretches where the underfooting is quite spongy and duff-covered, making for easier walking than one would expect.

Bend around your first bay just as you turn the corner to wrap around Ash Campground. Traverse around the second bay and cut across a point sticking into the lake, and come to Balsam Campground.

Keep following the shore, veer inland and go north of an unnamed lake, and come back to the shore and Pine Campground. This campground sits next to a marsh. Remember that May and June are the worst months for bugs, especially blackflies and no-see-ums.

Clark Lake Trail takes a southeast route along the shore. You have noticed by now that there have not been any real climbs, just a pathway that rolls over the landscape. A portage goes 0.3 mile northeast to Crooked Lake, which could make for a side trip.

Continue to follow Clark Lake Trail along the lake's edge and encounter another portage that connects Clark Lake to Loon Lake. This 0.2-mile portage takes you up and over a small hill and could make for another side trip.

After passing the portage, the trail turns southwest and intersects with the Fisher Lake Trail, which goes south. This is not used by canoers and is a lightly used hiking trail. From here, cross a low marshy area and encounter your first real uphill climb, about 70 feet in elevation. You will be moving westward, away from Fisher Lake, toward Whitefish Lake. Keep your eyes peeled for the next intersection, which will be on your right. If you miss it, you will end up on the shore of Whitefish Lake, but not before going down into a gully to cross a small creek. If this happens, turn around and look for your trail 0.2 mile from the stream crossing. Heed this piece of advice!

Once you find you are on the right track and heading north, you will pass between

Old bark trees dwarfs its human visitors

Hay Lake and Glimmerglass Lake. You will not see these small lakes, but will cross over a portage that connects the two. Descend back to the shore of Clark Lake, pass Maple Campground, and look for another side trail. This trail would go east to Birch Campground, but you will want to head northwest in order to stay on the Clark Lake Trail.

Hug the shore and climb the side of the embankment and come down to Cedar Campground. Pass the campground and drift through a large marsh inland. When you come back to the lake, look to the north, and see that you are almost done! The beach and canoe access are near where you started.

Find yourself at the end of your trip as you progress into a maintained picnic area. Just follow the shore to the canoe access and the parking area.

18

Craig Lake Loop

Place: Craig Lake State Park

Total distance: 7.5 miles

Hiking time: 4–6 hours

Gradient: Mostly moderate, some short difficult stretches

High points: Wilderness setting, moose, geology

Maps: USGS 7.5' Three Lakes, Craig Lake State Park; North Country Trail #12

Amenities: Two cabins for rent, rustic campground, backcountry camping, canoeing

Footwear: Backpacking boots

Pets: Not recommended

SUMMARY

Craig Lake State Park is the most remote state park in the Upper Peninsula. Canoers and hikers have weaved a myriad of trails through its wilderness setting over the years. With the coming of the North Country Trail (NCT), there is now a defined, well-used, and mostly marked passageway circumnavigating the lake. Canoeing is a popular activity in the park.

The land that is now Craig Lake State Park was originally purchased by Fred Miller—of Miller Brewing Company fame—in the early 1950s. Mr. Miller used the area for hunting and fishing, building several cabins and a lodge. The property was sold to a logging company upon Miller's unfortunate death in a plane crash in 1954. Michigan State Parks acquired the land in 1966.

There are no major climbs or descents. Half of this hike is on old forest roads, which are flat or rise and fall gently over the landscape. The only "real" trail is at the north end of the lake, which is rooty and rocky but easy to follow. Well maintained, all the intersections are marked with signs or YOU ARE HERE maps, keeping your confidence high for such a wild area.

ACCESS

Reaching the park is something of an adventure. Vehicles with a high clearance and 4x4 are recommended. However, if there has been a lack of rain for a period of time, even a small economy car can reach the trailhead by proceeding slowly and carefully. From Marquette, drive west on M 28. Eight

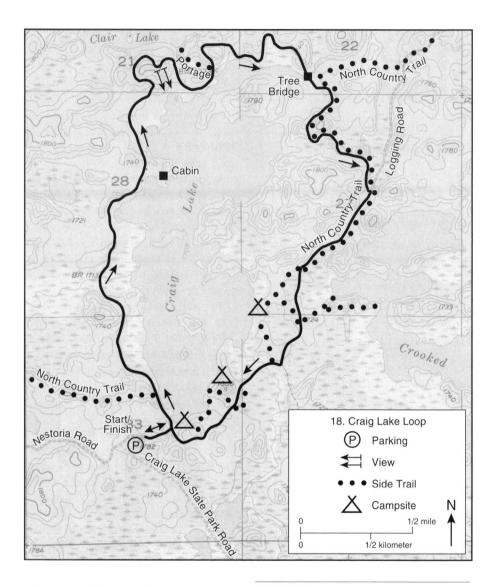

18. Craig Lake Loop

- (P) Parking
- ⇄ View
- • • • Side Trail
- △ Campsite

N

| 0 | | 1/2 mile |
| 0 | | 1/2 kilometer |

miles west of Van Riper State Park, look for a small, nondescript sign for Craig Lake in the right-of-way. Turn right, and the road is a maintained gravel road, although only 1½ cars wide, for 4 miles. At the intersection for Keewaydin Lake Road, veer left onto Craig Lake State Park Road (a rough, one-lane, cobblestone road) and drive 3 more miles to the trailhead.

THE TRAIL

From the parking area, start downhill on a gated gravel road. At 0.1 mile, your first intersection is with the North Country Trail. This is the location where you will end today's hike. Continue to your left, clockwise, following the NCT. Craig Lake Trail and the NCT share the same route for about half the hike's length. You will start out walking a very short stretch of the NCT, leave it for a considerable distance, and rejoin it on the northeast side of the lake after crossing the Peshekee River. Upon reaching the lake, you will see a rustic campground with fire pits, pit toilets, and a canoe launch. This is where your ties to civilization mostly end. Continue on the gravel road you will pass about 2 miles from the parking area. The road is the only access for those renting the cabins up the trail. Campground users must hike in.

The majority of your walk will be through second-growth northern hardwood forest. One would expect massive pines or hardwoods, but this is not the case except in a few rare instances. Get to know the sugar maple—you will see thousands of them on your journey.

Keep your eyes open for wildlife: loons, pileated woodpeckers, squirrels. Of course, you are in bear territory as well. The moose, a member of the deer family most hikers never see in Michigan, is resident in the park. Moose prefer hanging out in wetlands and along the lake's edge. Your route will be mostly inland, coming to the lakeshore only a handful of times. Take every opportunity to scan for these massive mammals.

The NCT splits to your left and heads west from Craig Lake Trail about 0.2 mile from the campground. Continue on the gravel road into the woods, losing the view of the lake. There are no trail markers on this portion of the trail but there no reason to have them yet. There will be need of them soon enough!

Take note of the numerous boulders and some rock outcroppings to your left, uphill. Cross an outlet drainage to the lake near the 1-mile mark. In dry years, the water is stagnant. The trail makes a slow climb after crossing the drainage, and there are more boulders and the trees are getting larger, especially white pine and yellow birch.

At 1.8 miles is a modern cabin on the edge of the lake. Only 0.2 mile up the trail is another cabin. At the second cabin, walk up to the outhouse, then follow the treeline to your right for about 50 feet and enter the woods and prepare for a rooty and rocky trail surface. Notice a massive white pine stump, just after you enter the woods, while you're still within sight of the cabin.

If you are visiting the park alone and wisely brought your whistle or other sound maker, now is a good time to pull it out and put it to use. There are many blind corners, hidden turns, and narrow passages through thick undergrowth until you reach the other side of the lake and pick up an old logging road.

Although rooty and rocky, the trail is in great shape, well worn, and well maintained. However, it is still unmarked. There are not any real climbs or descents for a fair distance. You will experience walking through a cedar swamp complete with corduroy road and find your very first trail marker, an orange diamond.

Three miles into your hike, experience your first real elevation gain of about 60 feet to the top of a rock outcropping, giving you a southward view of Craig Lake. Less than 0.2 mile farther and downhill, cross the portage that takes canoers between Clair Lake and Craig Lake. Descend and cross a small footbridge and find yourself at the bottom of another rock face. It appears that a social trail has been made going straight at the base of the formation. Look to your left and uphill for an orange diamond. It seems that these diamonds, although few in number, are placed in key locations. Hike up the backside of this geological formation, which can be slightly difficult at times.

After this second overlook, head back down toward lake level and turn east, making a descent that can be moderately

Craig Lake

difficult in places. Squeeze between the rock face and a thick alder swamp that has encroached onto the trail. Again, this is an appropriate time to find an orange diamond.

Head up and over a rib that comes off the backside of the formation and find yourself at the Peshekee River crossing. A YOU ARE HERE sign boosts your confidence, assuring you are not wandering aimlessly down the North Country Trail. Your "bridge" across the river will require some skill as you will balance yourself walking across an old, downed tree.

The NCT comes in from your left, merges with the Craig Lake Trail, and becomes marked with both orange diamonds and painted blue rectangular blazes.

The trail cuts across a point jutting into the lake, and the ground mostly levels out with some low spots for the next 0.5 mile. For the next mile, climb and descend several knobs. Between these knobs lies a low cedar swamp. You will descend the last knob using a rib before merging with an old log-

ging road. Apparently, the NCT folks ran out of paint, as there seems to be only the occasional orange diamond from this point on.

The two-track is level and rather straight. Just 0.3 mile after it becomes a two-track, the trail comes to another YOU ARE HERE sign directing you to campsites on Craig Lake. Continue following the North Country Trail along the old logging road.

Although you may not see moose, bears, or wolves in the park, look for their tracks and scat. Moose tracks look like enlarged white-tailed deer hoof marks, 5 inches in length. Moose scat resembles a cow patty. Bear tracks have long, padded heels, and bear scat can resemble grape preserves or be encrusted with insects, depending on what the bear has been eating. Wolf tracks and scat are very similar to those of a dog, except that the pad is not symmetrical like a dog's, and the scat contains fur.

Enjoy skirting a bog about 0.2 mile past the canoe portage, complete with tamarack, black spruce, Labrador tea, and leatherleaf.

A few hundred feet after leaving the bog, you'll spot a side trail heading to Craig Lake and campsites. The trail swings inland for a couple hundred feet, moves toward a foot-bridge, crosses a small stream, and turns back into the woods as a logging road.

Climb up and over a small saddle to your left, then bend to the right and level out in a westward direction. A small incline up and you have reached the intersection with the entrance drive. Turn left and return to your vehicle.

19

Fumee Lake Loop

Place: Fumee Lake Natural Area

Total distance: 4.9 miles

Hiking time: 2–3 hours

Gradient: Flat

Highpoints: Birding, rare plants, wide-open trails

Maps: USGS 7.5' Norway; Fumee Lake Natural Area

Amenities: Picnic area, artesian well, pit toilets, interpretive signs

Footwear: Tennis shoes

Pets: Yes

SUMMARY

The 1,800-acre Fumee Lake Natural Area contains a maze of trails that weave their way around 500-acre Fumee Lake. Established in 1992, this natural area is mostly unknown to the hiking community outside of the Iron Mountain area.

This Dickinson County park was paid for by the residents of the county when they overwhelmingly passed a bond measure to acquire the area for use and preservation as a natural area. Although the park is located very near Iron Mountain, a bustling tourist town that acts as a launching point for outdoor adventurers, users will be hard pressed to hear the hustle and bustle, as Fumee Lake sits in a low area, sheltered by hills and forests.

Both Fumee Lake and Little Fumee Lake are undeveloped, providing more than 5 miles of natural shoreline. The area was once used as a groundwater reservoir, and many buildings and an abandoned railroad grade remain. Since the area was little used and off limits for many years, the habitats have matured, and Fumee Lake Natural Area is home to many rare plants and animals.

Bald eagles and common loons are routinely seen. Seventeen species of orchids have been identified, along with three threatened plant species: walking fern, purple cliffbrake, and marsh grass of Parnassus.

Local schools use the area as a living ecology laboratory. Bring a pair of binoculars, as the bird life is quite diverse and plentiful.

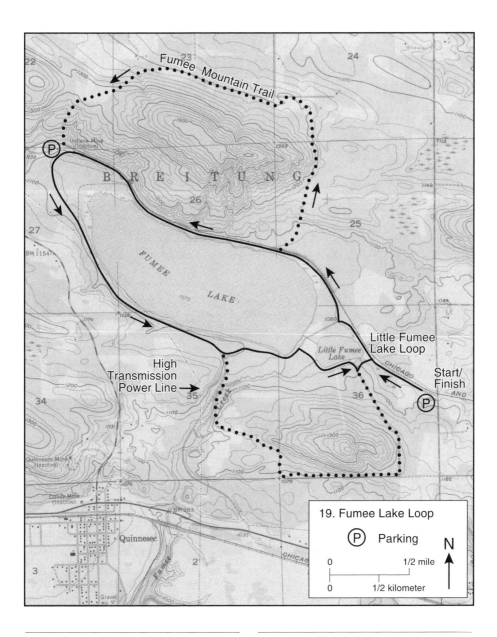

19. Fumee Lake Loop

P Parking

N

0   1/2 mile

0   1/2 kilometer

ACCESS

From Iron Mountain, take US 2 east 5 miles, and turn north onto Upper Pine Creek Road. The entrance drive to Fumee Lake Natural Area is marked on your left in 1 mile.

THE TRAIL

Although there are numerous trails for hiking, skiing, biking, and even snowmobiling, it is hard to get lost, as the Big Fumee Lake loop is on abandoned roads, very wide, and very

Maturing forests surround Fumee Lake

straight. At each intersection, a very useful YOU ARE HERE map keeps you on track.

The parking lot is large, which is indicative of the area's popularity. Look for a YOU ARE HERE sign at the farthest point from the where the access drive enters the parking area. Tread straight ahead, and you will have marsh on both sides of an abandoned road. Right away, start bird watching. Look for a belted kingfisher perched on the end of a branch, and listen for the soft and repeated "coo-coo-coo, coo-coo-coo" of the black-billed cuckoo, which may be hiding in the shrubby swamp.

At 0.2 mile the walkway splits. Continue to the left, where a shroud of thick shrubs shields your view from Little Fumee Lake. Fishing is not allowed in either lake: the county administrators respect the Michigan Department of Natural Resources determination that the lakes have a remarkable and unique fishery. The populations of small-mouth bass, rock bass, bluegill, pumpkin-seed, northern pike, brown bullheads, and yellow perch have lived in harmony for decades without human interference.

At 0.5 mile, the path splits again, and continues in a counterclockwise direction on level footing and a wide trail, lined with trees of nearly every variety. It won't take long to identify red, sugar, and mountain maple, speckled alder in the low areas, balsam fir, white and red pine, and paper birch. Less common trees are basswood, hemlock, ironwood, yellow birch, and even black cherry.

The trail comes into close proximity of the lake, and at 0.9 mile, it comes to the Fumee Mountain Trail trailhead. This is a one-way trail. If you choose to take it, start heading north at this point. It is 1.5 miles long and ends when it comes back to your current trail at the northern trailhead, located at the west end of the lake. Your view of the lake is mostly obscured by trees, and you are considerably higher than the lake's surface. There are two observation points where the canopy opens up enough for views of Fumee Lake.

At 1.9 miles, the lake becomes marshy and there is a small pond at the bottom of the hill. At 2.6 miles are a second trailhead and parking. Because several trails come into this area, pay attention to the signs and the YOU ARE HERE maps.

Once back onto the Big Fumee Lake Loop, you will find an artesian well just past the trailhead. Head back into the woods, which has become quite swampy. Numerous ferns, cedar trees, and occasional black ash sprout from the mucky soil. At 3.1 miles, leave the swamp, rise slightly in elevation, and notice the more open habitat. A low layer of shrubs is the only barrier between you and the lake.

Common loons require lakes with little or no human disturbances in order to nest. Look for loons and their babies, possibly riding on their backs, out in the open waters of the lake. Other water birds include common and red-breasted mergansers, pied-billed grebes, and great blue herons.

South Ridge Loop comes in from the right at 4.2 miles. Bear left, and at 4.5 miles is another marsh. Expect common yellowthroats, swamp sparrows, red-winged blackbirds, kingbirds, and gray catbirds to be flitting and singing in the area.

At 4.3 miles, turn right onto the Little Fumee Lake Loop. Little Fumee Lake is on the left, cloaked by shrubs and trees. Stride into an open field, which is an intersection for the South Ridge Trail coming in from the right, at 4.7 miles. Continue straight, uphill, and you will recognize the beginning of your outing, which has now become the end. Turn right and hike 0.2 mile back to your vehicle on the abandoned road.

20

North Country Trail: Trapp Hills

Place: Ottawa National Forest

Total distance: 34.1

Hiking time: 3–5 days

Gradient: Very difficult

High points: Exquisite views, rugged topography, remoteness

Maps: USGS 7.5' Bergland NE, Matchwood NW, Oak Bluff, Rockland; NCT MI-13, MI-14

Amenities: Remote wilderness; trail shelter at Victoria.

Footwear: Backpacking boots

Pets: Not recommended

SUMMARY

Backpacking in the Trapp Hills is not for the faint of heart. Although you are not in Colorado climbing a fourteener, this portion of the North Country Trail is as good as it gets for ascents and descents. This amazing journey can take the average backpacker four days to complete. If you have the time, take your time. You will lose count of the breathtaking views, the gut-clenching climbs, and the perilous descents.

This section of the North Country Trail is deep in the Ottawa National Forest. There are no services for miles in every direction. Take solace knowing that you are surrounded by nature as far as the eye can see.

The hills are primarily basalt, a very dense volcanic rock that emerged onto the scene billions of years ago. When the glaciers passed through, this highly resistant igneous rock resisted the miles-thick glaciers and was simply smoothed by the passing ice. Today, thin soil coats the surface, which means many roots protruding, so watch your step.

You must exercise caution due to the active logging in the area. My father and I spent the better part of an afternoon bushwhacking through the forest after we came upon a significant logging operation that had obliterated the trail. Thankfully, this was at the very end of our toil, but the party that was keeping track of us had been instructed to call the Michigan State Police if we had not emerged from the woods at our predetermined time. Of course, this is always recommended—you should always tell someone where you are going and when to expect you back. We were 15 minutes late and were greeted by a note stuck in the trailhead sign on the edge of the road. About a half hour later, we were greeted by a state trooper. She dutifully noted in the record that we were only late, not lost.

This area of the national forest is crisscrossed by US Forest Service roads and a few county roads. All are gravel. Some are in great condition, but others, such as Victoria Road, can be a horrendous nightmare after heavy rains.

ACCESS

Depending on how much time you have or how far you wish to hike, there are several options. The western trailhead is off M 64, just south of White Pine. There is a grass parking area for about four cars. The eastern trailhead is at Victoria, which is on Victoria Dam Road. Access is from Rockland, on US 45. In between, you can use trailheads on Norwich Road, and on Victoria Road about 2 miles east of Norwich Road (keep in mind that this road can be a rutted mess). USFS 222 has roadside parking and so does Old M 64. No user fees were in place for the trail as of this writing.

THE TRAIL

Day 1

Pulling into the parking area, you will get the feeling that your hike will be challenging, staring at the 700-foot high "hill" crowned with pines and hardwoods. Marked with blue diamonds (eventually changing over to blue painted rectangles), the trail is faint, but skilled backpackers experienced with these conditions should find their way. The majority of this hike is through mature and maturing northern hardwood forest, with some open balds on the tops of hills.

The first 2.9 miles are between M 64 and Old M 64. After a grueling, 700-foot climb to the top of the hill and the Bergland fire tower (no access allowed), gently saunter downhill through the woods to Old M 64 and a roadside parking trailhead. The trail, after crossing Old M 64, immediately climbs back up, reaching elevations approaching 1,740 feet. It is on this forested hill where you will have your first view of the Trapp Hill landscape. Look west for the checkmark formation that adorns the top of Copper Peak. That would be the flying ski jump, about 30 miles away.

For the next 25 miles, you'll wind feverishly around these wooded mounts. Enjoy the scenery, for tremendous effort will be required to reach the vistas.

Trekking another 0.8 mile downhill through mature hardwood forest, you will cross USFS 326 and quickly negotiate your way up and over a 200-foot-high hill. From here, it is 9.3 miles until your next road crossing. Meander southeast, and at the base of the hill by an intermittent stream is the terminus of the Gogebic Ridge Trail. Continue uphill, and as you embark northeast, enjoy the view of the valley below.

From this point, you will follow the escarpment for about 3 miles until you descend to cross the Soo Line Railroad at the 9.8-mile mark into the day's hike, and Bush Creek 0.2 mile farther along.

When crossing the river, be aware that this may be your last chance for water for the next 16 miles, so load up. This may be a great place to camp for the night, but you may want to move inland 0.25 mile or so, since the area is swampy, and mosquitoes could be voracious in the summertime.

Day 2

After the previous day's 10-mile hike, a quiet night's sleep miles from a paved road and

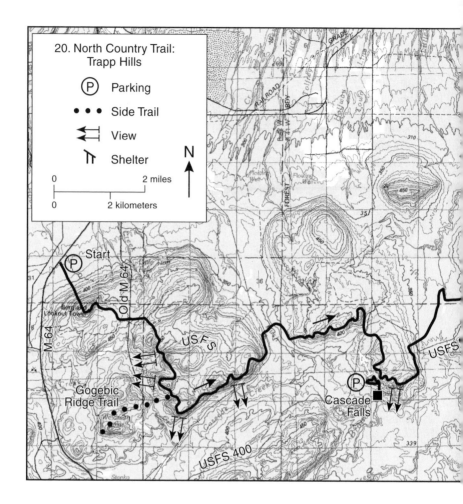

surrounded by the Ottawa National Forest should recharge your batteries. Break camp and be sure to trek back to Bush Creek to load up on water. There will be a few intermittent and small stream crossings, but in dry years they may be empty.

The hike starts as a gentle uphill grade, then quickly gains in steepness, and you are back hiking along the escarpment at 1,400 to 1,500 feet in elevation. At 2 miles comes your last vista for a while as you make a hairpin turn along the north side of this small knob and start a steep downhill plunge for

1 mile to your next road crossing. About 0.1 mile from USFS 400, cross an intermittent stream.

A small pond is located in a swampy area just north of your current position. The basic routine of your hike continues, climbing up and then hugging an escarpment, and at 1 mile from the road, you'll be at your first overlook, just after crossing a two-track. Hug the precipice for another 1 mile, bending from a southeast to a northwest direction. The decline takes about 0.3 mile, then it is a 1-mile march to the north along the

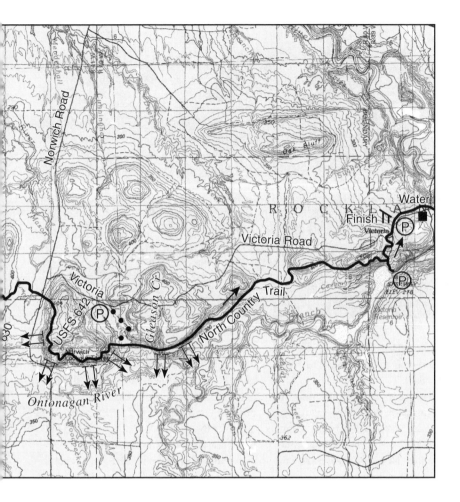

contour. In the last 0.1 mile you'll descend to USFS 630.

A pleasant respite from the rest of your hike, your course will remain flat for the next 3.7 miles. About 1.5 miles from USFS 630, cross an intermittent stream and turn from a north to a southeast direction through some wet ground, and bend to the east. One more intermittent stream crossing is 0.1 mile from the paved Norwich Road. Camp near the stream. Plan ahead and make a water drop just up the trail before your hike, in case this stream is dry.

Day 3

Sleep in, rest your weary body, and from here, your direction of travel parallels Victoria Road. On a good day, it is a rugged gravel road. After a few spring rains, it is a nightmare passable only by the bravest of souls with a four-wheel-drive vehicle. With this in mind, you could make a loop using the NCT and loop back on Victoria Road.

Your easy hiking will cease as you trudge uphill 250 feet and resume walking along the edge of an escarpment, weaving up and over several outcroppings of granite. At the

Trapp Hills

2-mile mark, cross USFS 642, which is gated and little used—you may hike right by it and not even notice it.

Carry on while paralleling the edge of the West Branch of the Ontonagon River, which is in view through the trees several hundred feet below. At 3 miles, start a descent to Whisky Hollow Creek, a reliable stream at the 3.9-mile mark. Just 0.1 mile beyond is a spur trail to Victoria Road, 0.8 mile away. Past this point is a considerable stretch of private land, where trailside camping is prohibited. Make camp at this point, letting the background noise of the creek lull you to sleep.

Day 4

Pack camp and plod uphill onto private land, back up to the edge of the abyss holding the Ontonagon River. Your first overlook is at 0.5 mile, and you'll cross Gleason Creek at the 2-mile mark.

From this point, the face of the granite will slowly decline in elevation for the next 3.5 miles. When you reach the bottom of the hill, the landscape will be flat as you bend north, then start an eastward climb uphill 250 feet in elevation. Keep putting one foot in front of the other along the crown of the granite formation, through mature northern hardwood forests. At the 7.5-mile mark, start downhill and you'll reach a gravel road that leads between the town of Victoria and the Victoria Dam holding back the West Branch of the Ontonagon.

Parallel the road for less than 0.1 mile, head back uphill, and cross Victoria Road at 8.5 miles. Negotiate around a hill with a communication tower adorning its crest, and start a downhill jaunt to the Old Victoria Townsite, which is part of the Keweenaw Heritage Sites. For a nominal fee, you can take a tour of the log homes, which have been restored to their former glory. They were used by miners and their families in the 1890s. There is parking at the townsite, and a trail shelter is just off to the east of the log cabins at the 10-mile point in your hike.

21

Overlook Trail

Place: Fayette State Park

Total distance: 1.4 miles

Hiking time: 1 hour

Gradient: Mostly moderate

High points: Views from escarpment, historic village, rare hardwood forest dominated by cedars

Maps: USGS 7.5' Fayette; Fayette State Park map

Amenities: Visitor center, modern campground, interpretation

Footwear: Hiking boots

Pets: Yes

SUMMARY

Fayette Brown had a great idea.

During the heyday of iron mining in the Upper Peninsula, Brown, general manager of the Jackson Iron Company, noticed that he was going to great lengths and cost to ship his iron to the lower Great Lakes to be processed. He built a furnace at Fayette, which is considerably closer to the iron mines.

In 1866, Fayette was chosen because of the protected bays, plentiful limestone, and readily available hardwood nearby to run the two blast furnaces and charcoal kilns that were built.

Around this industrial site lived 500 residents, and with them came the amenities of the day. Stores, baseball fields, churches, and even an opera house operated here. Many of the workers emigrated from as far away as northern Europe, bringing with them their cultures and customs.

In 1891, the town ceased after producing more 200,000 tons of iron. The buildings were left behind and the people moved on, leaving Fayette a ghost town. The State of Michigan acquired the site in 1959, creating a 750-acre state park, which attracts over 100,000 visitors yearly.

The Overlook Trail takes you up to the edge of the escarpment, but not until after a short history lesson. This lollipop loop begins at the interpretive center. After seeing the sights, you will be drawn to the historic village and all the stories it will tell.

Although Fayette State Park is known for the story of the blast furnaces, its overlook

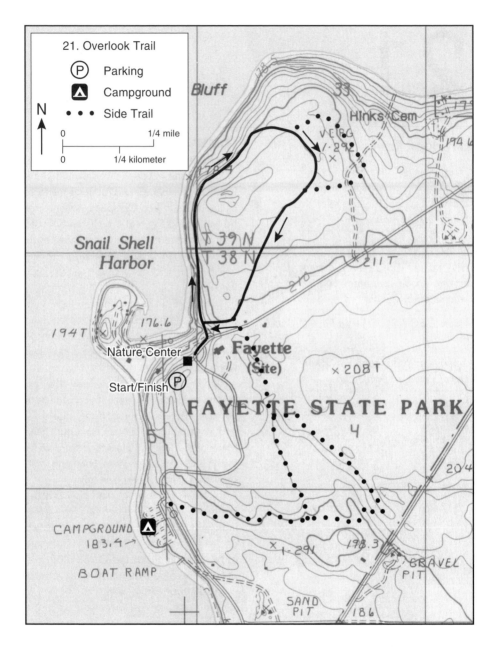

21. Overlook Trail

- ⓟ Parking
- 🔺 Campground
- • • • Side Trail

N

| 0 | 1/4 mile |
| 0 | 1/4 kilometer |

Bluff

33

Hinks Cem

Snail Shell
Harbor

T 39 N
T 38 N

194T

176.6

Nature Center

Start/Finish ⓟ

Fayette
(Site)

× 208 T

FAYETTE STATE PARK

CAMPGROUND
183.4 →

BOAT RAMP

× 1-291

198.3

GRAVEL
PIT

SAND
PIT

186

trail immerses you in a natural setting once common but now rare in the Upper Peninsula. Before loggers and abundant deer, many of our forests were dominated by white cedar, which now grow again on top of the Niagara Escarpment, the rock formation that creates the falls of the same name.

View of Limestone Cliffs from Historic Village

ACCESS

Fayette State Park is located on the Garden Peninsula. Take US 2 west from Manistique to Garden Corners and go south on M 183 for 17 miles. Take the park's entrance drive to its end and park at the visitor center. The trail starts to the right of the visitor center.

THE TRAIL

Your path starts as a paved walk as it descends to a gravel road, which you will need to take uphill to your right—a moderate climb. Take the road about 0.2 mile uphill to an intersection marked by a post marked with a number 1, which also includes a YOU ARE HERE map.

From this grassy field, turn left and head uphill to get to the edge of the escarpment. The substrate is crushed gravel and very wide. You will notice the abundant cedars,

absent from most of today's northern hardwood forests.

On your left, an interpretive sign overlooking Snail Shell Harbor and the historic town site tells the story of how local residents used to skate across the ice to Escanaba in the winter. Looking to the horizon, you can just make out the ancient lake level on Burnt Bluff just south of your current location. On the right is a concave land formation indicating the Post-Algonquin Glacial Great Lakes stage. To the left of this formation, a small dip in the landform shows an even higher and older Lake Algonquin shoreline.

Carry on, moving into a thick forest, composed mostly of cedar and paper birch. Rock outcroppings on your right, some the size of a small house, line the upward slope of the hill. The trail peels away from the escarpment and heads uphill with a moderate climb for a couple hundred yards. Your cedars diminish and the forest takes on a typical northern hardwood character, with sugar maples and paper birch.

The ground cover is noticeably different. Look for sarsaparilla berries and "doll's eyes" in the late summer and early fall. Take note of a few American beech trees in the forest. This is about as far west in the Upper Peninsula you will find this gray, smooth-barked tree.

Narrowing considerably and changing to a light path in grass, your trail takes you under a thinning forest canopy which lets in more light. A large patch of red-berried elderberry, a species you are recommended not to eat—the berries are mildly poisonous to humans—is found in one of the forest openings. You should not feel that these are going to waste, though, as the local birds feast on the fruit when it becomes ripe.

You'll reach trail marker #3 near the top of the hill, 0.4 mile from your first intersection.

At this intersection, you can veer left for a 0.5-mile loop or right for 0.3 mile. Both bring you back to the main trail. Stroll to the right and you will have a slight climb through the forest. The trail levels out and continues through the grass.

The 0.5-mile loop merges with your trail, coming in from behind and to your right. Although the state park map indicates that this is the location of marker #4, in fact it is just an old, blue-tipped post with a footprint carved into it.

The trail descends slowly back toward the town, and you will notice that the woodland is once again dominated by cedars, as it was at the beginning of your hike. Keep your eyes open for white ash, an uncommon tree in this forest.

Your "missing" trail marker #4 is 0.2 mile downhill, at the edge of a mowed right-of-way along the entrance drive. Look to your right, and you will see the gravel road you used to reach marker #1. Walk downhill and enjoy the history lesson.

22

River Trail

Place: Van Riper State Park

Total distance: 3.8 miles

Hiking time: 1½–2 hours

Gradient: Easy to difficult

Highpoints: Overlook, moose habitat

Maps: USGS 7.5' Champion, Michigamme; Van Riper State Park map

Amenities: Modern campground, beach, picnic areas, fishing

Footwear: Hiking boots

Pets: Yes

SUMMARY

Van Riper State Park is the only state park in Marquette County, Michigan's largest. It was just a few miles east of here where iron ore was discovered in 1845.

There are several hiking trails in the park; one is Miners Loop, where you can see evidence of pit mining. The River Trail parallels the Peshekee River, the same Peshekee that has its origins in Craig Lake State Park. This trail is a lollipop loop. The stem is flat, while the loop is quite rooty and rocky and can be difficult to climb in some places. However, your efforts reward you with a view of Lake Michigamme and the surrounding landscape shaped by ancient mountains and more recent mining.

If you are going to see moose in the Upper Peninsula, this is a prime location, and the straightforwardness of accessing their habitat makes your adventure an easy one.

ACCESS

Van Riper State Park is 25 miles west of Marquette on M 28/US 41. After passing the main entrance road (get your park permit here if you do not already have one), there is a trailhead immediately on your right. Drive past this trailhead and, just before the bridge crossing the Peshekee, turn right onto an unmarked gravel road and park to the side. Walk up the gravel road, which is being developed into future campsites, until you reach the trailhead sign for River Trail.

If you are short on time, continue west on M 28 to Huron Bay Road and turn right.

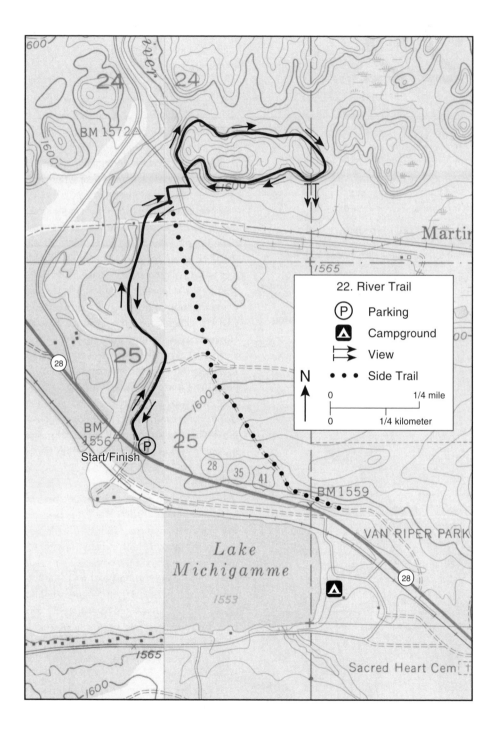

24   24

600

BM 1572 A

1600

river

1600

Martin

1565

22. River Trail

Ⓟ Parking

🏕 Campground

├──▶ View

• • • Side Trail

N

0   1/4 mile

0   1/4 kilometer

28

25

1600

BM
1556
Start/Finish

Ⓟ

25

28   35   41

BM 1559

VAN RIPER PARK

28

Lake
Michigamme

1553

🏕

1565

Sacred Heart Cem

1600

Peshekee River

At the first gravel road, turn right, cross the river, and trailhead parking is on your right. If you have more time, park at the trailhead across from the park entrance and take Old Wagon Road Trail to River Trail.

THE TRAIL

The trailhead is marked, and after walking between a couple of conifers, you'll see the pathway immediately splitting into two treads. Taking the left corridor, you'll come to a bench overlooking the Peshekee. A short spur trail to the water's edge will tempt you to try your fishing skills in the Peshekee.

Many mature red and white pines make up the forest canopy along the edges of the river. Sugar and red maples are also present, but in no great numbers at this point. Bending to your right, the other trail comes back and merges with your wide and well-maintained trail.

In 1985 and 1987, 59 moose were transplanted from the Algonquin National Park in Ontario to a release site just north of Van Riper State Park. Walk slowly, deliberately, and quietly, and keep your eye on the river's edge below. Moose consume vast quantities of vegetation, and the soft rushes and sedges on the banks of the Peshekee make a veritable buffet for them.

The River Trail continues to parallel the slight curvature of the waterway, with a very gentle uphill rise. You will reach the top of a hill at 0.7 mile, where the forest becomes mostly red pine. Keep your eyes open for signs of past forest fires. There are many charred red pine trunks, but the trees seem to have survived the blazes that swept through this forest.

Peel away from the river, bend around to your right, and start a gentle descent at 0.9 mile. At 1.2 miles, Old Wagon Road Trail comes in from your right, making a perpendicular intersection with River Trail. Turn left onto the remains of this old road. and 0.1 mile later reenter the woods, cross a small stream, and you can see the remains of the wagon road going straight into the woods. You will bend right, walk under some electric transmission lines, reenter the woods, and come to a gravel road and map kiosk 0.2 mile from the bend.

Even in dry years, mosquitoes and their brethren can be voracious, since you are so close to standing water. Even at high elevations and in dry habitats far from water, make sure to prepare for biting bugs.

Checking your park map, you see the word "overlook." This is a reality check that at some point, you are going to start climbing. After crossing the road, you will start your climb in earnest. It's moderately steep to start, but you will soon be reacquainted with the roots and rocks that make up so many of the Upper Peninsula's trails.

After a short distance, you will come to another split in the trail. Continue clockwise along the Peshekee while admiring the rock outcroppings on your right; the river is on your left. Mosey along the contour for 0.3 mile, up the backside of your hill toward the overlook. Notice that this part of the forest has switched over to mostly sugar maple.

Though your path is virtually devoid of trail markers, an orange metal diamond appears to warn you about your uphill climb. This is a difficult climb, but not quite a scramble, for the next 0.2 mile straight up the back of the hill.

At the top, notice a bowl-shaped formation in front of you. At the backside of the bowl, 0.9 mile from the last the trail intersection, is a large lip, which is your overlook. Turn to the right, then head up the side of this lip to your vista.

In the view of the valley below, Lake Michigamme is off to the right. Looking downhill, you'll see rock outcroppings and boulders. Parallel the edge of the overlook as you work your way back toward the intersection to complete your lollipop loop.

You will walk the circumference of the overlook, inland from the edge with no views. Then traverse some depressions and use some saddles to get around some higher ground. When the earth flattens out to a slight undulation, look for a bench near an overlook. It was situated here for hikers coming in the other direction. For you, it means your descent is about to start.

In the background, you can see the Peshekee through the canopy. In front of you is a staircase made of local rocks and large timbers to make the descent a little easier on the ankles. This moderate to slightly difficult trail descends quickly to the intersection.

If you choose to loop counterclockwise, the trail would be an abrupt ascent and a gradual descent, versus our chosen route of a gradual climb and a sudden decline.

23

Shakespeare Trail

Place: John Henes Park

Total distance: 0.5 mile

Hiking time: 1 hour

Gradient: Flat

High points: Plant diversity, unique landscaping, birding

Maps: USGS 7.5' Birch Creek

Amenities: Urban park with picnic facilities, swimming beach

Footwear: Flip-flops

Pets: Yes

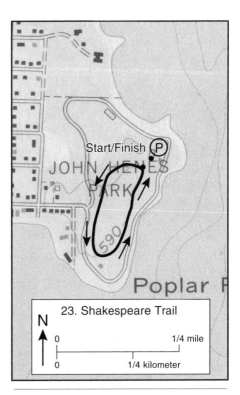

23. Shakespeare Trail

N

0   1/4 mile

0   1/4 kilometer

SUMMARY

John Henes gave the park that bears his name to the citizens of Menominee on September 30, 1907. Henes donated the park when the area was heavily industrialized. Henes loved trees, and these old-growth specimens reminded him of his German homeland and motivated him to preserve this park.

Famed landscape architect Ossian Cole Simonds (of Detroit's Palmer Woods fame) designed the park using natural landscaping. Today, we take for granted incorporating

Shakespeare Trail

natural features into our landscape designs. At the turn of the last century, the philosophy was much different, and designers often moved large amounts of soil to create landscapes. Simonds would have none of that. He designed the park's original paths using water features, winding trails, and the large trees. Most of these designs have been lost over time due to fires and design changes made since.

Henes Park has a sandy swimming beach, playgrounds, picnicking, and colorful ponds. On a false island that juts into Lake Michigan, the looped hiking trail is surrounded by the mile-long park circle drive and all the amenities that come with a modern park. A main loop is accessed by numerous spur trails. Heavily woodchipped and flat, this is more an opportunity to explore than a determined march.

This city park is on a 50-acre peninsula jutting out into Green Bay. Similar to

Marquette's Presque Isle Park, the Menominee version is smaller and flatter. Beyond the elaborate entrance arch, the paths are named after famous authors.

Leave the boots in the car, as this level trail system can be managed in flip-flops.

ACCESS

From Menominee, take M 35 north and turn right onto 44th Street. Take 44th Street until it ends at the park entrance. Take the one-way road and park at your first shelter. A trail spur starts immediately behind the shelter. Look for woodchips.

THE TRAIL

With all the accesses to the loop trail coming out to the entry drive as spurs, this can be a very confusing experience. When you come in from an access trail and come to an intersection, stay to the right until you get back to your starting point. Although you still could get lost, that is a relative term, as you are surrounded by a one-way road on a very short trail.

Heavily forested and lush, John Henes Park is home to an abundance of tree species, ferns, flowers, and just about anything green. With the contrast in forest colors, the woodchips, the landscaping, the several fountains, and even a manmade stream, you might expect to see the Mad Hatter run out of the woods at some point. Even if he does not, this park seems surreal, like a fairytail land. The maze of trails are all named after well-known authors and poets, including Whittier, Longfellow, Goethe, Shakespeare, and Byron.

Even at the end of summer, the animal life, especially birds, is far more plentiful than what one would expect. Chattering chickadees, nighthawks, gulls, loons, mergansers, squawking great blue herons, nuthatches, leaping frogs, and scattering squirrels probably use this patch of habitat as an oasis in a sea of humanity. Off in the distance, the paper mills belching steam into the air and the roar of traffic probably drive wildlife to this sanctuary.

If you do lose your bearings, be adventurous and take a path that looks unfamiliar to you. If you come out to the circle drive, double back and trek in a new direction. Interpretive graphics identifying trees will help you keep your bearings. There are small ponds, large ponds, low areas, massive trees, and ferns crammed into low, swampy areas, most of which are smaller than 10 acres in size. Cedar, basswood, dogwood, bigtooth aspen, paper birch, sugar maple, rose twisted stalk, false Solomon's seal, and rue anemones are just a few of the plants you may identify, even late in the season.

After you have found your way out of the woods, explore the natural cobble and sandy beach.

III

Land of Hiawatha

24

Songbird Trail

Place: Au Train Lake National Forest Campground

Total distance: 2 miles

Hiking time: 1–2 hours

Gradient: Easy

High points: Guided audio tour of trail, observation tower

Maps: USGS 7.5' Au Train

Amenities: Rustic campground

Footwear: Hiking boots

Pets: Not recommended

SUMMARY

What if I told you of a surefire, guaranteed way not only to see wild birds up close, but identify them as well?

The next time you are traveling across the Upper Peninsula on M 28, stop in at Au Train Grocery on Forest Lake Road in the center of Au Train, just west of Munising. The turnoff for Au Train is marked on the highway.

Walk in, and ask the storekeeper for the Songbird Trail kit. For a $10 deposit ($8 will be returned) you will be handed a pair of binoculars, a tape recorder, tape, and a field guide. Scoot on down to the Au Train Lake National Forest Campground on the south end of Au Train Lake.

There is an observation tower, and the 2-mile loop is sprinkled with bird identification signs. Put in the tape, and at each sign, you will play the corresponding bird's call.

Keep your eyes open, listen, and keep your hat on. The hat is not for the sun (well, okay, it could be) but to keep these birds from bombarding you in the head! You are perceived as an invader, as you are playing the territorial call of another male. This recording will elicit a response, the male will defend its territory by coming out into the open, calling, and possibly buzzing by your head in order to get you to leave!

This wander through the woods truly integrates hiking with wildlife watching. The idea is that you investigate these habitats using tape recordings of birds played at identified locations to attract songbirds.

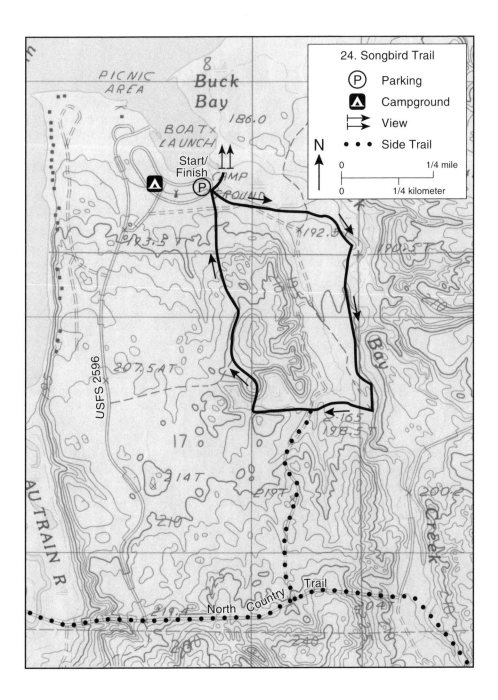

It works—sometimes too well. It is an impressive sight to watch a bird weighing about an ounce taking on a full-grown human!

Twenty species are featured, from the very common American robin, red-winged blackbird, and black-capped chickadee to the hard-to-find least flycatcher, black-throated blue warbler, and winter wren. This is a great way especially to get kids excited about bird watching.

ACCESS

From Munising, take M 28 west, and turn south onto H 03. Au Train Grocery is in Au Train, which is found shortly after turning south on H 03. Continue on H 03 south, turning east on County Route 550. The entrance to the national forest campground is about 0.75 mile on the left. Take the campground entrance road until it ends. Park across from site #11 and get your kit ready, for the fun is about to begin.

THE TRAIL

Mosey into the hardwood forest of red maple, balsam fir, and hemlock. You will notice that the ground cover is a sprinkling of clintonia and woodfern.

Within 50 feet, you'll reach a spur trail to an observation area overlooking Buck Bay, part of Au Train Lake. A modest boardwalk leads you to the foot of the 20-foot tower, which gives you a nice view of the bay and the surrounding marshlands. Back at the intersection, make a left turn, and get the tape player ready. Your first bird, the American robin, is not the most exotic or rare of Michigan birds, but play the tape, listen, and watch. If you have no success, do not fret, there are many other birds to taunt with your tape player. Each species has a different breeding season, and results will vary

depending on the time of year. Probably the overall best time would be the beginning of June. However, this method of attracting birds should work from mid-May through July.

The forest floor is a little rooty and rocky, so pay attention if you are walking and taunting the birds at the same time. Your next bird, along the edge of a shrubby swamp, is the red-winged blackbird, which is territorial. You would be, too, if you had to defend up to ten nests attended by females caring for your young.

There is a well-used, well-maintained path, and along with the plastic blue diamonds attached to the trees, your confidence will remain high. Common yellowthroat and black-capped chickadees are your next quarry, then a bird that many birders only hear and rarely see, the winter wren. A close relative, the house wren, gives a rapid three-noted *TWEEDLE-Tweedle-tweedle* that descends the musical scale but maintains its volume and intensity. A winter wren has the same notes, but goes up, down, and all around while sounding five to 15 notes. Winter wrens like nesting in uprooted trees, many of which are present in these woods.

Good luck with the next bird, Michigan's largest woodpecker—the pileated. Their territories are hundreds of acres in size, so you need to be in the right place at the right time to spot the bird that was the inspiration for Woody Woodpecker. You may not see a pileated woodpecker in these woods, but you should spot the next two birds on the interpretive signs, the black-throated blue warbler and the veery, both of which prefer forests with large trees. There is even a bench between the two interpretive signs.

Begin to parallel Buck Bay Creek at 0.5 mile. This is a trout stream, but it's tangled

Buck Bay Creek

with fallen trees, and only careful anglers would dare risk losing their lures here. Admire the large cedars leaning over the creek. Some approach 2 feet in diameter.

Hairy woodpeckers, cedar waxwings, and white-breasted nuthatches are the birds featured at the next three stations. You will encounter large yellow birches while continuing your walk along the creek. At 1 mile, make a hairpin turn to your right, which takes you out of the creek valley and into an open field. A worn sign, directing you toward the North Country Trail, sits on the edge of the field. The sign points to a spur trail that is little used and isn't even on the official North Country Trail (NCT) maps anymore. It's a good idea to bring a compass and a good topo map with you if you want to venture the 1 mile to link up with the NCT.

Follow the edge of the woods and reen-

ter the forest, which is mostly sugar maple. Surprisingly, there are a fair number of black cherry trees and even some American beech.

Heading west, pass the ovenbird interpretive and come to a bog, signed "Grass Pink Bog" on your right. Although this would be a great place to play the call of bog residents like the white-throated sparrow or the olive-sided flycatcher, there are no interpretive signs here. Follow the bog as you bend to the north at 1.3 miles.

Climb up and over a small hill, play the Eastern wood pewee recording, and continue to saunter over small knobs and depressions through the landscape as you head north back toward the campground. Your next bird may get a head start on you before you reach its sign. Listen for a whistled and often-repeated *Here I am! Where are you?* The red-eyed vireo, once the most widespread forest bird in Michigan, drops its calls all summer long from high up in the canopy. You may need to be extra patient to lure this bird down low enough to see its olive color and bright red eyes.

Next comes the least flycatcher, which unlike the red-eyed vireo makes its quick, nondescript *che-beck* call in the spring, then becomes very quiet.

You will travel about 0.3 mile—a noticeable gap—until your next sign, for the blue jay. At this point, you are about 0.1 mile from the end of the hike, and you can see the campground through the forest. There's a station for one more bird, the yellow-rumped warbler, and you will come back to the trail intersection and parking area. Hopefully, you still have your hat.

25

Rivermouth Trail

Place: Tahquamenon Falls State Park

Total distance: 14.7 miles

Hiking time: 6–8 hours

Gradient: Mostly easy with some moderate climbs and descents

High points: Remoteness, sweeping views, moose

Maps: USGS 7.5' Timberlost, Emerson; Tahquamenon Falls State Park map; NCT MI-09

Amenities: Lower Falls has a modern campground and concession area. Rivermouth Unit has a modern campground.

Footwear: Hiking boots

Pets: Not recommended

SUMMARY

Over half a million guests visit Tahquamenon Falls State Park each year. The most popular trail is the Falls Trail (Upper to Lower Falls), attracting tens of thousands yearly. The Rivermouth Trail, however, attracts only a fraction of the park's visitors.

This is a wild walk that should take the better part of a day to complete. Mostly flat, it traverses through maturing forests, old clearcuts, swamp, and even crosses a large marsh using a bridge. The hike is mostly high and dry with a few opportunities to view some wild lakes and it does meet the river at the end of the hike.

This may be only the second location in Michigan where you will have a fair opportunity to see moose. They inhabit the low marshes toward the end of your hike, before you come to the poor dirt road, Tahqua Trail.

You'll see many habitat types, everything from thick swamp and expansive marshes to old fields where massive pines used to stand, lakes, streams, and second-growth forest.

Although the sign at the trailhead says 11.7 miles to Rivermouth Camp, due to reroutes of the North Country Trail, your hike is slightly longer.

ACCESS

The eastern trailhead is at the Rivermouth Unit campground. From Paradise, take M 123 south 3 miles to the park entrance. Park behind the contact station. The western trailhead is at Lower Falls, which is 10 miles west of Paradise on M 123. Drive to

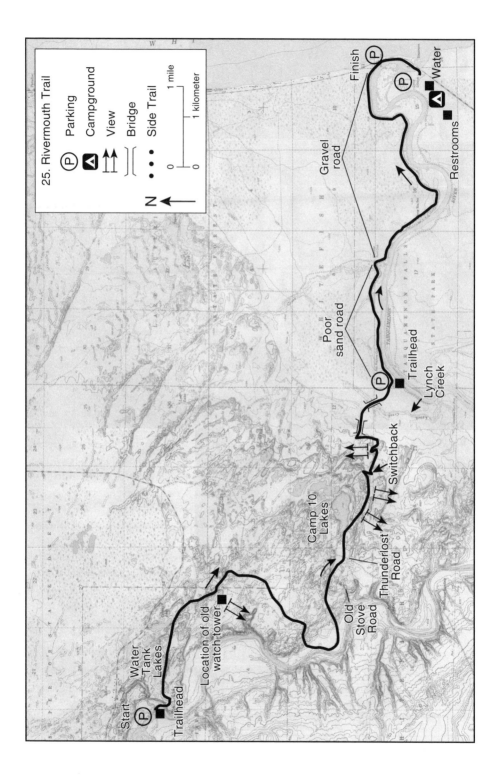

25. Rivermouth Trail

P Parking
△ Campground
↑↑ View
〔 Bridge
• • • Side Trail

0 ——————— 1 mile
0 ——————— 1 kilometer

N ←

Start
P
Water Tank Lakes
Trailhead
Location of old watchtower
↑↑
Camp 10 Lakes
Old Stove Road
Thunderlost Road
Switchback
↑↑
↑↑
P
Trailhead
Lynch Creek
Poor sand road
Gravel road
Finish
P
P
Water
△
Restrooms

Lynch Creek is a good place to find moose

the end of the park entrance road, which ends at the parking lot. Walk toward the amphitheater all the way to the left-hand side of the day use area and look for the North Country Trail. A sign indicates the Rivermouth Trail at the top of a staircase.

THE TRAIL

You'll be using a segment of the North Country Trail that receives only a fair amount of foot traffic, although it crosses a very busy state park. Start your hike by entering the campground while keeping to the right, counterclockwise on the campground loop, until you reach the trailhead, marked by a large sign and a North Country Trail logo. Don't be fooled by the sign. Recent trail rerouting has extended the length of this hike. The sign says it is 7.1 miles to the Tahqua Trail, when it is really 8.9 miles. And, it says 11.7 miles to the Rivermouth Campground when it really is 14.7 miles.

Now that we've added some extra mileage to your hike, take a deep breath and take the stairs downward to the Tahquamenon River and immediately use a small footbridge to cross a little feeder stream. Take a second deep breath, maybe two, as you'll scramble up a steep hill to get to the top.

Take a breather—this will be your only major, steep climb of the day. Think of this summit as weeding out the less than brave day users to the park. Enjoy the habitat up here, which is mostly mixed red pine, white pine, and jackpine. The ground cover consists of bracken ferns and blueberries, making a late summer hike a tasty one.

Trek eastward and enjoy the many small ascents and descents rolling over the landscape. The path is well used and marked adequately with blue blazes as it cuts through the moss, leaving a sandy underfooting. This will be the prevalent tread surface through your hike.

At 0.9 mile, skirt by Water Tank Lakes, affording you a downward view of several small bodies of water. Be careful accessing water here, as it is rather marshy around the shore. The trail follows the ridge along the lakes, peels away to the southwest, and in another 0.2 mile, it will zigzag to the top of the highest point in the area, where a watchtower once stood. All that remains are the cement footings and the remains of the steel legs formerly set into the concrete. On most days, the view is obscured by the weather, influenced by Lake Superior, which is less than 10 miles away.

Descend this knob and you will walk a ridge that falls off to both sides. The trail will continue to lose elevation, until it sinks into a valley flanked on both sides by forested hills that parallel the trail, which has become very straight and wide, until you come to Farkas Road 0.2 mile later.

Although there is a trail sign at this intersection, there is no indication of the name of the road. If you turned north on Farkas Road, it would be 1 mile to M 123. Farkas Road is a two-track negotiable by most vehicles.

Cross the two-track into the woods, and continue southeast, then south, then southwest. The habitat is young, mostly jackpine savanna. Some maps show you crossing a two-track within 0.5 mile of Farkas Road. If this does exist, I have missed it both times I've hiked this trail.

The topography is rather flat as you curve through the landscape, then you'll start hiking on a ridge and see a varied landscape on both sides. At the top of what appears to be another local high spot, the forest thickens with white spruce, and you'll take a steep drop down and head west toward the Tahquamenon River.

The trail turns into a two-track after about 0.5 mile of hiking through white spruce and red maple forest. This two-track is scantily marked with blue blazes in this area, but the trail is wide and easy to follow. Until your next road intersection at Timberlost Road, this will be the case. Just stay on the two-track until you reach the intersection with Old Stove Road (the name of the two-track you are on) and Timberlost.

Unless someone told you, you would not know that you are only about 200 yards from the Tahquamenon River. Obscuring your view is a thick forest of red maple, hemlock, and white spruce. However, a few feeder creeks give away that the mighty Dark Waters is nearby. Stand still in the forest and feel its presence.

The two-track will turn from a southward to an eastward direction and climb up and out of the river basin into an open savanna. On your right is a large ridge. About 0.1 mile after leaving the forest and entering the savanna, the trail intersects with Timberlost Road. A sign for Old Stove Road is stuck in the ground at the base of—you guessed it—an old stove that has seen better days.

Leave the two-track and walk northeast, diagonally up the side of the ridge and you'll be between some boggy seepage wetlands and swamps on your right and Camp Ten Lakes on your left. You'll notice that the trail blazes have been placed more frequently here. This ridge continues to climb in elevation, becoming the predominant geological feature on the landscape. Eventually, you are above the treetops to the right, with thick forest on your left obscuring any view that may be left of Camp Ten Lakes.

The southern face of this sand ridge is unforested. Again, on most days, the view is obscured by the weather, but if it isn't, you will have a wide, expansive vista of the forest to the south.

Approach a set of switchbacks, bringing you down about 100 feet in elevation to follow another sand ridge. Climb another knob, which, again, appears to be the high point in the immediate vicinity. The trail lumbers downhill to a ravine, where there is a stream crossing on a small wooden bridge.

Negotiate the stream and head north back into the woods for about 0.2 mile, then drop in elevation to what appears to be a water-inundated two-track. Never fear—although this localized flooding is caused by nearby beaver activity, the trail has been locally rerouted onto drier footing. The forest is thick, but suddenly ends at the edge of a massive beaver dam, a major engineering feat. Thankfully, the local trail volunteers have built a nifty boardwalk on the top of the dam. Take a moment to survey the scenery: this expansive wetland, produced by the local beavers, may be your best opportunity to see a moose.

Reenter the forest, and about 0.2 mile later, cross Lynch Creek on another footbridge. A much smaller wetland, this may be another place to spot the largest member of the deer family. At over 1,000 pounds, moose are a force to be reckoned with. If you keep a keen eye out, you may find their 5-inch-long hoofprints in soft ground. A better sign are their cow patty-like droppings. Since they eat aquatic vegetation, their stools tend to be sloppy, so watch your step!

The trail become flat, straight, and wide, marked with the official painted blue rectangles of the North Country Trail. The footpath ends 0.5 mile from Lynch Creek at a trailhead on Tahqua Trail. There is parking for about three cars.

Turn left (east) and follow the Tahqua Trail 5.7 miles to M 123. Turn south and walk the road 0.7 mile to the contact station at Tahquamenon Falls Rivermouth Unit. Walk the forested Tahqua Trail, marked by painted blue rectangular blazes, past numerous private residences while taking the time to enjoy one of the several pullouts overlooking the Tahquamenon.

26

Blind Sucker River Pathway

Place: Lake Superior State Forest

Total distance: 6.7 miles

Hiking time: 3–5 hours

Gradient: Mostly moderate with a few challenging climbs

High points: Views of the Dead Sucker River valley, blueberries in season, walking view of Lake Superior

Maps: USGS 7.5' Grand Marais NE; NCT MI-09

Amenities: Trail traverses three rustic campgrounds with potable water, pit toilets

Footwear: Hiking boots

Pets: Not recommended

SUMMARY

You need to be a little brave, because this Michigan state forest pathway is lightly used and in a somewhat remote area. This loop parallels the Dead Sucker River, rising and falling over the landscape, mostly through dry forest and marsh. When the Blind Sucker Trail meets with and shares the North Country Trail, the combined trail heads northward toward Lake Superior through what appears to be even drier forest and alongside some logging operations. Cross the county road and head to Lake Superior, where the forest feels more boreal. You'll hike parallel to the lake for about 2 miles through the Lake Superior State Forest Campground, eventually crossing back over the road to your starting point.

This is a remote area with no surface water access between your vehicle and Lake Superior, so prepare accordingly. The low and swampy areas along parts of this hike are also prime bear habitat, so leave Fido with someone else, and make your presence known, by talking with your hiking partner or to yourself if you're solo.

ACCESS

From Grand Marais, take H-58 east. The pavement ends once you cross into Luce County, and the road becomes County Route 407. Five miles from the county line, turn south into Blind Sucker #1. The trailhead parking is marked. If you continue on CR 407, Blind Sucker #2 is on CR 410 about 2 miles farther down the road.

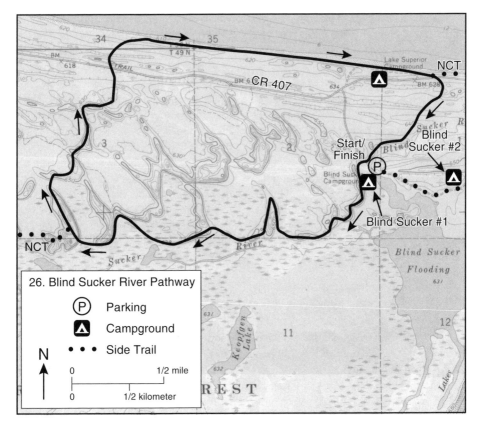

26. Blind Sucker River Pathway

(P)	Parking
⛺	Campground
• • •	Side Trail

N

0 —————————— 1/2 mile

0 —————————— 1/2 kilometer

Start at either Blind Sucker #1 or Blind Sucker #2. The trailhead is officially at #2, although it makes your journey a lollipop loop. To save yourself some time (mostly by not driving an extra 4 miles), park at the marked trailhead parking at #1.

THE TRAIL

At the Blind Sucker #2 campground, there is a sign with an overview of the area. Starting out on a flat and wide path, maneuver through sandy soils and a small grove of pines and shrubs. This spur trail leads between Blind Sucker #1 and #2 campgrounds, and is about 0.2 mile from the trailhead to the bridge atop the dam over the Blind Sucker River. The impoundment behind the dam is the Blind Sucker

Reservoir, which offers fishing for bass and bluegill.

Cross the bridge, and note the parking area on your right. Veer left and follow blue circular blazes into campground. The trailhead is on your right between a couple of campsites. Pass between the happy campers and immediately clamber up a moderately steep hill.

Hike up a blueberry-covered ridge. The trail is wide and well used. The forest habitat is very dry, comprised mostly of white pine, jackpine, red pine, and some paper birch. There are some bracken ferns among the blueberry bushes. When you reach the top, the trail will turn left. You will be following a sand mound of sorts, more of an esker than a ridge. On your left, until you reach the intersection with the North Country Trail, will be the Dead Sucker River Valley. On your right is mostly forest with some occasional swamps.

Continue clockwise, and your sand esker turns more into an embankment, and you will be walking its edge. Through the sparse white spruce, red pine, and jackpine, you will be afforded spectacular views of the river valley. The wide, unspoiled view makes you feel more like you are in Alaska, not in Michigan.

The maturing forest is showing a few more red oaks, but its sandy soil still only allows red pine and some white pine to dominate. White spruces are sparse and not of any great size.

About 0.8 mile from the campground, the trail becomes more lightly used. Overhanging bracken ferns and blueberry bushes will make it difficult to find the path at times. However, the blue blazes will be your beacons leading you through the forest.

Descend to the edge of the river valley in order to traverse a swampy area on a boardwalk and, as soon as you've crossed the boardwalk, you head back up to a sand esker that continues to parallel the river valley. The habitat becomes mostly jackpine-dominated, dry northern forest in this stretch, while the swamp is mostly black spruce and cedar swamp with some spirea.

By this point, you will notice that you may be the first person to step on this trail in days. Keep checking the ground for footprints. Instead of Nike and Merrell, look for fox, coyote, deer, and maybe even bear or wolf tracks. You are truly in a wild area.

The Blind Sucker Trail continues to taunt you—will I be on a sand ridge or following the edge of the river basin? You will occasionally turn inland away from the view of the river basin. On the first turn inland, keep your eyes open for signs of a past forest fire. There are several scarred trees, some still living, from a fire that passed through many years ago.

A puncheon boardwalk is underfoot as you enter a black spruce and cedar swamp. While the ground is rather flat here, soon after the swamp ends, make a steep climb back up to the top of the sand ridge you have become accustomed to traversing.

By this point, you have been swatting mosquitoes and deerflies. Although you may be in a very dry habitat, you are close enough to the breeding grounds of these pests that they'll still be a problem. As you swat, you can still see through the trees to the river basin.

The trail takes on the appearance of a two-track, and at about this point your river basin is more of a marsh. The thread of the stream has been swallowed up by scores of sedges. A lake shown on the map is dry—the only sign of its past glory is the desiccated muck that once lay at its bottom. The two-track peels off into the woods and becomes a trail again.

Keep your eyes on those blue blazes, which appear more frequently now, as the trail itself is barely noticeable on the ground. Another 0.2 mile farther along, black spruce and white cedar swamp is on the left, and a sandy hill on your right, while the mosquitoes continue to be voracious. The pathway on the ground has disappeared, but the blue blazes are frequent and your confidence should remain high. Keep the swamp on your left and the hill on your right, and the mosquitoes will follow. The path does reappear on the ground after you leave the swampy area and climb a primitive wooden staircase to the top of the sand hill you have been following.

After a 60-foot climb, your reward at the 3-mile mark is a picnic table and the intersection with the North Country Trail. The

Dead Sucker River

view is wide and sweeping; this spot has become a popular primitive campsite, for obvious reasons.

Descend down the backside of the hill, leaving the views of the river basin behind. The blazes have become blue rectangles, the North Country Trail standard. The habitat continues to be dominated by red pines and jackpines, known as dry northern forest. At the bottom of the hill, cross an ORV trail 0.2 mile from the intersection. Soon after, find yourself merging with a two-track. You will need to pay attention here, as the hiking trail will split off to the right and is heavily blazed to draw your attention to this fact.

You can measure this course not by its length, but by the number of times you need to retie your shoelaces! The brackens and blueberries overhanging your feet tear at your boots nearly the entire length of your excursion. In late summer you can grab a tasty treat as compensation for having to stop so often.

Climb slowly as you move across the contour of the landscape on the faint path, which is surprisingly easy to follow using the blue blazes. Stay with the blazes as you approach a seed tree cutting on the left. Parallel the clearcut for about 100 yards into the woods, which has become mostly jackpines with a ground covering of lichens. As you continue to the north, the terrain flattens out.

It is amazing that even so close the earth's largest freshwater lake, you are essentially walking through a desert-like area.

After an eastward bend in the trail, the canopy opens up, and the landscape continues to get drier in appearance, with sparse jackpines. Even the bracken ferns are struggling for moisture. Up and over this ridge, you will be back in a thicker, more mature forest. A clearcut will appear on your right and hug the edge of the forest until you reach CR 407.

Crossing CR 407, it is a straight, northward shot 0.3 mile until you reach the Lake

Superior shore. The trail is perched on the edge, where the forest meets the sandy beach and dunes. The habitat has considerably changed, to paper birch, white pine, and red maple. The ground is covered with mosses and bearberry.

Turn east and parallel the Lake Superior shore, and enjoy the mostly flat ground. About 1.5 miles from where you first reached the shore, the trail turns inland slightly and you'll face several small ascents and descents before returning to the edge of the forest and the view of the lake.

Greet campers at Lake Superior State Forest Campground as you walk the entire campground between their campsites and the edge of the lake while still in a forest setting. The trail brings you up and onto CR 407 for 0.1 mile. Look for the circular blue blazes leading you away from the North Country Trail and back 0.6 mile toward the Blind Sucker Campgrounds. The trail allows you to revisit the dry jackpine and red pine forests, then climbs up and over a small hill for your final descent into Blind Sucker #1, and the bridge back to the trailhead is on your left.

27

Chippewa Trail

Place: Indian Lake State Park, South Shore Unit

Total distance: 1.3 miles

Hiking time: 45 minutes

Gradient: Easy

High points: Cedar swamp, undeveloped beach

Maps: USGS 7.5' Manistique West; Indian Lake State Park map

Amenities: Modern campground

Footwear: Tennis shoes

Pets: Yes

SUMMARY

During wetter times after the glaciers retreated, Indian Lake would have been called Indian Bay, as it was connected to Lake Michigan until its water level dropped. Today, it is the Upper Peninsula's fourth largest lake at 8,600 acres. Although large, it is not very deep, averaging less than 15 feet in depth.

Indian Lake State Park was acquired in 1932, and the Civilian Conservation Corps (CCC) built many of the structures in the park, which still stand today.

Experience a northern swamp as this nature trail skirts around and through a habitat that most would never venture into. Although the footing may be muddy in the spring or after rains, it is mostly passable during these times and dries out by midsummer.

ACCESS

From Manistique, take County Route 442 4 miles to the west. The park entrance is on your right. After the contact station, turn left, taking the road toward the day use area. Turn left at the parking area, and park all the way at the end of the last parking lot. The trailhead is between the lot and the boat launch.

THE TRAIL

Heading clockwise, you will be greeted by a young forest thick with white spruce. The ground is covered in partridgeberry, goldthread, mosses, and young balsam firs. This wide, well-maintained trail is flat overall, since you will be in a swampy area. There

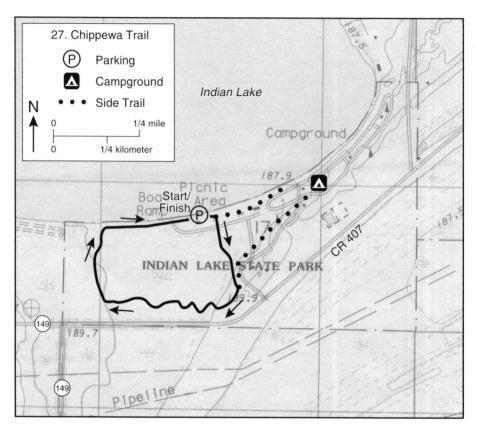

27. Chippewa Trail

Ⓟ Parking

🅰 Campground

••• Side Trail

N

0 ———— 1/4 mile

0 ———— 1/4 kilometer

Indian Lake

Campground

187.9

187.5

Picnic Area

Start/Finish

Boat Ramp

Ⓟ

🅰

CR 407

187.9

INDIAN LAKE STATE PARK

189.9

149

189.7

149

Pipeline

are some exposed roots and no trail markers leading the way. Thankfully, there are trail maps with "you are here" designating your location at intersections.

Your first intersection at 0.25 mile is uphill from the parking area. Drier in habitat, this area has some towering white pines. Notice some larger red pines and paper birch and even some balsam poplar. You are a few hundred feet from the county road and its roar of traffic.

Notice your trail made of crushed gravel as it parallels the county road. The vegetation thickens as you leave the dry habitat and twist toward a noticeably swampier environment. Typical wetland species, such as speckled alder, elderberry, and swamp thistle are sure signs that you are in an Upper Peninsula swamp. Be grateful that you are

on a well-used trail near civilization, not deep in some impenetrable mire.

Continue to wind as you turn north, and 0.4 mile from your last intersection, cross a bridge over a small creek, parallel it for 0.1 mile, then cross back over again and follow the right bank. Surrounded by cedars, you'll notice the tea color to the water. The cedars and mosses stain the water with tannic acid when they decompose. Not to worry, tannic acid is the component that gives your iced and hot tea its color. Ask backpackers what they think of tannic acid-stained water. Most will tell you it's tasty because it is usually high in mineral content.

Wind has blown down a few large trees, opening up the canopy and allowing black ash to attempt to fill the void. As you bend away from the creek toward the right, Indian

Lake becomes visible through the thick forest. As you approach the water, a natural sand beach comes into view but quickly loses out to the encroaching forest. Cedars perch right on the edge of the lake, preventing any attempt by nature to create a sandy beach.

Your footing is slightly elevated and dry due to the sandy substrate. Although you are only 10 feet from the lake, the cedars make access difficult. However, these trees act as a natural blind for viewing wildlife. If you are lucky, mergansers and wild ducks will be floating a mere 20 feet away on the lake.

You are nearing the end of the hike when you see buoys indicating a no-wake zone around the boat launch. Cross over the boat launch parking area to a paved trail, and immediately turn right at the first intersection back onto a well-worn path, and in 100 feet, you'll be back to the parking area.

28

Gold, Red, and Blue Trails

Place: Carl A. Gerstacker Nature Preserve at Dudley Bay

Total distance: 2.4 miles

Hiking time: 1½–3 hours

Gradient: Easy to moderate

High points: Plant diversity, unspoiled beach, remote lake, rare plants

Maps: USGS 7.5' Albany Island, Prentiss Bay

Amenities: None

Footwear: Tennis shoes

Pets: Prohibited

SUMMARY

This 890-acre preserve, formerly known as Trout Lake Preserve, was renamed in 1996 after Carl Gerstacker, a founding member of the Michigan Nature Conservancy's board of trustees. However, the local Twining family originally sold parcels to the Conservancy to preserve the area around Little Trout Lake.

Over 4 miles of pristine Lake Huron shoreline showcase the three major types of natural beach found in Michigan: bedrock, sand, and cobble. Old dune ridges and beaches now host forests dominated by red maple, red pine, and white pine.

Although the preserve has magnificent frontage on the pristine lakeshore, the trail is inland through dry forested habitats. You can create a loop hike via the marked, moderately used trail system and part of the state highway. Explore the Gold Trail and turn west onto the Blue Trail, taking it to the Red Trail and continue west to the other trailhead and parking area.

Mostly in dry-mesic northern forest, you'll hike up and over old sand ridges, view a pristine inland lake, and enjoy migrating birds and butterflies in the forest and on the beach. Bring your flower guidebook with you, as there are several endangered species in the preserve worth identifying.

ACCESS

From St. Ignace, take I-75 north to M 134 (Exit 359) and head east 13 miles. There are two trailheads, one on each end. For the purposes of using this corridor, park at the east trailhead along the Lake Huron shore. Hikers

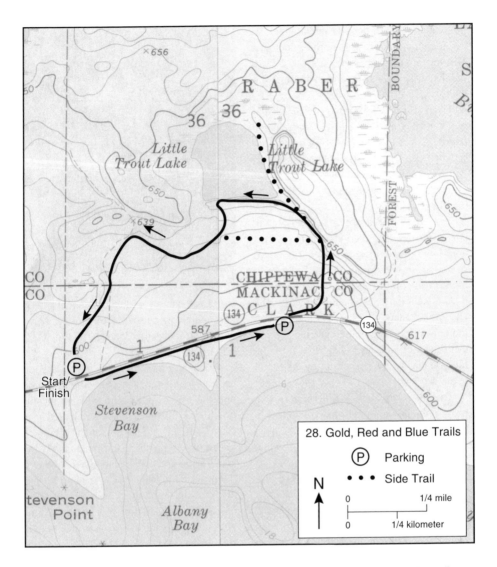

28. Gold, Red and Blue Trails

Ⓟ Parking

• • • Side Trail

N

0   1/4 mile

0   1/4 kilometer

are discouraged from using the sanctuary during bow and firearm deer seasons, as the Nature Conservancy permits deer hunting in the preserve. If you do hike during hunting season, wear hunter's orange.

THE TRAIL

At the trailhead, you will be drawn to the lapping waters of Lake Superior. Resist the urge until later, and walk east 0.1 mile on M 134 to the marked trailhead on the north side of the highway.

Skirt through a thin band of trees and walk another 0.1 mile through squishy footing under a power line to the east. Watch where you step! There are uncommon and even endangered plants underfoot, including grass of Parnassus and Houghton's goldenrod. Fringed gentian is also very common in this part of the sanctuary. This low area was probably a swale before the highway was built and disrupted the hydrology.

Head inland to the north on a thin trail that has a mostly sandy base. Ground juniper, bearberry, and bracken ferns take over as the ground dries and the trail enters the woods You will reach a gate and a trail map in another 0.1 mile. You will start by investigating the Gold Trail.

The woods here are a second-growth mix of deciduous and coniferous trees. This area has been logged in the past hundred years, so do not expect to see old-growth forest. The corridor widens considerably as it skirts an interdunal wetland on your right. Using binoculars, you can identify some of the flowers growing in the distance. Do not even think of walking in this delicate habitat—you may be swallowed up by the toothpaste-like marl.

The abundant pink lady's slippers that grow in the preserve will whet your appetite for uncommon flowers. Look for them sulking underneath the sunshine-stealing bracken ferns.

Come to a split in the trail at the 0.5-mile mark, where a post signifies your position at the intersection of the Gold and Red Trails.

Continue on the level Gold Trail, through more second-growth forest, 0.2 mile farther to an intersection that is discernible only by markers on trees, not by a post similar to the one you just passed. Blue markers continue to the left here, while the Gold Trail continues straight and will parallel the east side of Little Trout Lake. Turn left onto the Blue Trail.

Gradually walk up a ridge, gaining about 20 feet in elevation, and look through the trees and downhill for Little Trout Lake. Maintain your elevation on the ridge, and as

Fringed Gentian

you approach an uncharacteristically large and seemingly out-of-place hemlock, come across a social trail leading to the lake's edge.

About 0.3 mile from the previous intersection, your ridge starts to come to an end and the trail seems to go straight. At this point, look for an unmarked path (still the Blue Trail) going to the left, as the faint path ahead of you is a social trail that leads to the lake's edge and an intimate experience with a wetland. The Blue Trail is marked for hikers coming from the other direction, so make sure to peek over your shoulder once you start on what you think is the correct trail, which heads south. The Blue Trail winds up and over small sand ridges and sandy knobs, and through the bracken ferns and blueberry bushes.

At 1.1 miles, leave the canopied forest and find the post identifying the intersection of the Blue and Red Trails. Turn right onto the Red Trail, which appears to be an old road and winds toward the southwest. The trails are marked with plastic markers with the trail names on them, some with arrows denoting turns. The canopy thickens as you head off this old roadbed back onto a winding trail through the forest.

You will come out onto another old road 0.5 mile farther along, and turn left at another directional post. Instinct tells you to go right, but trust the post! This old road lasts 0.1 mile, then turns into the woods, and you should hear the occasional passing vehicle on the highway. The trail ends 0.2 mile farther at a sandy parking area and M 134.

Turn left (east) and take the highway back 0.6 mile to your car, and enjoy the unspoiled beach.

29

Horseshoe Bay Trail

Place: Horseshoe Bay Wilderness

Total distance: 2.5 miles round trip

Hiking time: 2–3 hours

Gradient: Flat

High points: Wilderness beach, migrating warblers

Maps: USGS 7.5' Evergreen Shores

Amenities: Rustic campground at trailhead

Footwear: Tennis shoes

Pets: Not recommended

SUMMARY

Leave the roar of I-75 and the scads of tourists in St. Ignace behind, and hike through wild cedar forests searching out the waves lapping on the Lake Huron shore. Its 3,790 acres dedicated in 1987, Horseshoe Bay Wilderness is part of the Hiawatha National Forest.

Keep your ears open and eyes peeled during late May for the peak of the spring bird migration. Their melodious songs are a cacophony of pleasant sounds. American redstarts are abundant, taunting you with their zigzag movements through the forest. Listen for the *teacher-teacher-TEACHER!* call of the seldom seen ovenbird. Even if you're only a casual birder, you're likely to see or hear at least 10 species of warblers alone.

Balsam fir becomes more prevalent than the cedars as you approach the beach. As the canopy starts to open, the ground underfoot will become sandy. The forest ends abruptly as you saunter out onto a classic, undisturbed sand beach. Look for a small creek struggling to empty its tannic acid-stained waters into Lake Huron as the big lake does its best to send wave surges upstream.

About 100 feet of grasses, wildflowers, and small shrubs separate the forest from the beach. Take solace in the knowledge that you could walk about a mile south and 6 miles to the north and still be on a beach unblemished by resorts, piers, and oil-soaked sunbathers.

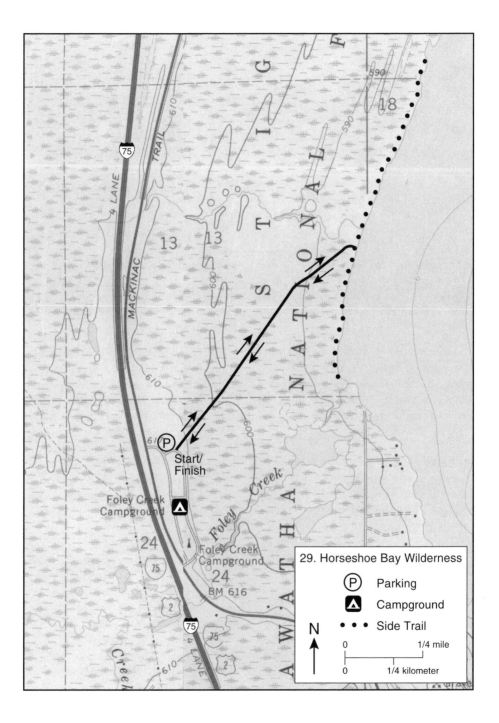

75

610

4 LANE

MACKINAC TRAIL

13

13

600

610

590

590

18

610

600

S T I G

N A T I O N A L

A W A T H A

610

Start/
Finish

P

Foley Creek
Campground

Foley Creek

Foley Creek
Campground

24

24

75

BM 616

2

75

75

75

2

Creek

610

4 LANE

2

29. Horseshoe Bay Wilderness

P   Parking

🏕   Campground

•••   Side Trail

N

0   1/4 mile

0   1/4 kilometer

Horseshoe Bay

Congregating offshore in season you'll see migrating waterfowl, such as common loons, northern shovelers, and mergansers. Keep your eyes open for coyote, bear, and even wolf tracks on the sandy beach in this 3,800-acre wilderness.

ACCESS

From St. Ignace, take Business I-75 north until it ends at Mackinaw Trail (H-63). Take Mackinaw Trail north to Foley Creek Campground. The trailhead is located in the campground at the farthest point from the entrance. For more information, call (906) 786-4062.

THE TRAIL

The 2.5-mile round-trip trail leading through the Horseshoe Bay Wilderness to the wild shores of Lake Huron is straightforward, wide, and relatively well used. This is usually not the case for a hike in a federally designated wilderness area. Do not let the wide,

woodchipped path and the hand-hewn logs placed over wet areas fool you. You are in a wild area that sees relatively little use.

The Horseshoe Bay Wilderness sees little human activity other than the occasional hiker who graces its paths. One would expect to labor under moderate-sized cedar trees through swampy footing. This is not the case: even in spring, the ground is mostly high and dry. Logs span the occasional wet spot over small springs and muddy areas.

The trailhead is marked by a sign indicating you are entering a proper wilderness. Again, do not let the wide and maintained footpath make you think you are in a well-used state park. You will likely have the forest and the beach all to yourself.

The forest starts out mostly as a dry cedar swamp. You will cross a small stream about 0.5 mile into your jaunt provided it is not an overly dry year. The trail continues wide and maintained for another 0.1 mile and becomes a little higher and dryer. Enter a proliferation of balsam firs lining your way for the next 0.75 mile.

The forest is rather thick but not very mature, as this area was logged around the turn of the 20th century. The poor soils make it slow going for a forest to rebound. At 1 mile into your walk, your footing becomes sandy as the forest opens up into a complex of red pines, then jackpines and a layer of bracken ferns. In the last 0.2 mile before you reach the beach the forest thins, then disappears at the mouth of a small creek. It's only a small, tannic acid-stained thread of water draining the swamp you just ventured through—this waterway doesn't even have a name on your map.

Standing on a wilderness beach, it's easy to ignore the resort at the water's edge a mile to the south. If you have the time, explore the cobbles, rocks, and plants such as silverweed poking up among the myriad stones for 7 miles to the north. Rambling northward in low-water years, you will be able to walk mostly on sandy and cobble beach. With high lake levels, your footing may be wet, as the onshore marshes can just blend into Lake Huron. In wet years, you would be better off exploring this shoreline by canoe.

Wildflowers grow right down to the beach, as there are few if any sunbathers to disturb them. As you walk north, the beach will become more cobbled. Adventure as far as you wish, noting that the mouth of the unnamed creek is your trailhead. Follow the trail back to your car.

30

Laughing Whitefish Falls

*Place: Laughing Whitefish Falls
Scenic Area*

Total distance: 1 mile round trip

Hiking time: 45 minutes

Gradient: Easy

High points: Waterfall, fern diversity

Maps: USGS 7.5' Sand River; NCT MI-11

Amenities: Picnic area, pit toilets

Footwear: Flip-flops

Pets: Yes

SUMMARY

Driving down the rutted, but passable, gravel road to the trailhead may be more of an adventure than the hike itself! In fact, the trail is in much better shape than the county road leading to this scenic area.

The 960-acre Laughing Whitefish Falls Scenic Area is for day use only. However, the number of cars in the lot may give you the impression that there are more people here than there really are, as this is a jumping-off point for the North Country Trail.

The wide, level path to an overlook and a staircase brings you to the bottom of Laughing Whitefish Falls.

ACCESS

From Munising, drive west on M 94, turning north at Sundell onto Dorsey Road. The paved Dorsey Road ends after 2 miles, and you are directed 0.5 mile down a rough gravel road to the trailhead.

THE TRAIL

From the parking area, skirt though a regenerating forest composed mostly of poplar, where the wide, crushed gravel trail keeps invading plants at bay. Once in the hardwood forest, take note of all the different ferns growing in the area: oak fern, woodland fern, common polypody fern, ostrich fern, cinnamon fern, and sensitive fern, to name a few.

Some notable wildlflowers include rose twisted-stalk and white baneberry. Spring ephemerals are numerous, as the leafless

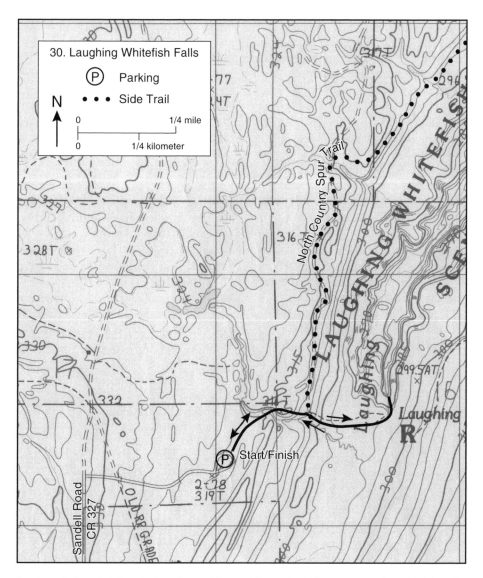

hardwood forest lets plenty of sunshine through, allowing these short-lived, but beautiful plants to develop during the very short growing season.

After you pass a second bench, the trail heads slightly downhill. Cross a stream and notice a two-track splitting to the right. You will stay on the crushed gravel trail as it bends to your left (east) with a slight down-

hill grade. When you reach a third bench, your pathway continues on a level grade, and the hardwood forest becomes dominated by maturing sugar maples. Ferns and wildflowers are still plentiful, making the forest feel full and lush.

On the north side of the trail, keep a keen eye open for the 1.9-mile-long spur trail that leads to the North Country Trail.

This spur is poorly marked and there is no trailhead sign. Since it is a lightly used footpath, you will have to keep a sharp eye open for the blue painted markers. The spur trail will be easier to find on your way back from Laughing Whitefish Falls, as it is just before the two-track.

In low-water years, you'll see Laughing Whitefish Falls before you hear them through the forest. The falls are relatively quiet, as the water flows over the hard, 450-million-year-old Au Train Formation, which sits atop Miners Castle sandstone, the same type of rock that makes up the famed Pictured Rocks. Actually, both formations here are forms of sandstone, but the upper, Au Train layer is more resistant to erosion than the lower layer.

Take a step back in time and descend the 100 stairs to the bottom. There is no direct access to the river, although many hikers have made their way through the barriers to comb for fossils in the layers of sandstone laid down by ancient seas.

On the way back up, take a break and admire the sandstone face, where lichens, liverworts, and ferns cling for dear life. These air plants get their nutrients from dust, pollen, and other aerosoled organic materials, while the tumbling falls provide the moisture they need.

After returning to the trail, if you choose to venture onto the North Country spur trail, you may be rewarded with a view of an unnamed and virtually unknown waterfall, although you will need to visit in the early spring or after a heavy rain, as it is created by an intermittent stream. The unnamed falls, where you will negotiate around a deep cavern, is about 1 mile north of the intersection. Although it is small, you will have this waterfall all to yourself.

31

Mackinac Island Loop

Place: Mackinac Island

Total distance: 8 miles

Hiking time: 4–5 hours

Gradient: First half is moderate with a few challenging climbs, second half is flat

High points: Views from an escarpment, wildflowers, history

Maps: USGS 7.5' Round Island, Evergreen Shores, St. Ignace; Mackinac Island State Park map

Amenities: Island has full services

Footwear: Hiking boots

Pets: Yes

SUMMARY

First settled by British troops in 1780, the 2,000-plus-acre Mackinac Island has not changed much over time. Automobiles were banned at about the time they were invented over one hundred years ago, Fort Mackinac still remains, and horse-drawn carriages are the main form of transportation.

The British colonized the island just a few years after we declared our independence, fearing that the Americans would invade Fort Michilimackinac on the mainland. This, of course, never happened, and the United States diplomatically took ownership of Mackinac Island after the war. In a surprising move, however, the British retook the fort during the War of 1812. Another round of diplomacy eventually returned the island to the United States. In 1875, Mackinac Island was declared America's second national park after Yellowstone, which had been established only three years before. The Department of the Interior relinquished federal jurisdiction to the State of Michigan, creating our first state park. (This makes for a great trivia question.)

Today, over three-quarters of the Mackinac Island is preserved as a state park. There are no camping facilities here, and all camping is strictly prohibited.

Although the vast majority of visitors to Mackinac Island stroll up and down Main Street sampling fudge, steering clear of horses, and dodging bikes, there are the rare few who venture onto the more than 50 miles of hiking trails on the island.

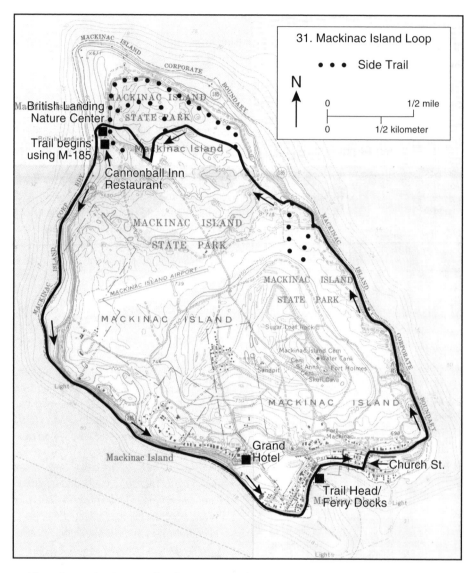

There is no circuit route that keeps you completely on pathways and off the roads of Mackinac Island. Nevertheless, walking the roads here (where the internal combustion engine is banned) is not the hair-raising adventure you would expect if hiking a state highway traveled by automobiles. In fact, M 185, the road where you will be laying

footsteps, is the only state highway in Michigan where you will dodge road apples, not road ragers.

Thread together some street strolls and hikes on the Manitou, Tranquil Bluff, Swamp Line, and British Landing Trails before returning to your starting point using M 185. Shops, eateries, and hotels dominate the

Mackinaw Bridge

south end of the island. However, Mackinac Island State Park is crisscrossed by hiking trails and both paved and gravel roads.

ACCESS

Unless you have your own airplane or Great Lakes–worthy boat, the primary access is via one of the three ferry companies out of St. Ignace or Mackinaw City: Arnold Transit Company (www.arnoldline.com), Shepler's (www.sheplersferry.com), and Star Line (www.mackinacferry.com).

THE TRAIL

From the ferry docks, take Main Street (also known as Huron Street and M 185) east, and turn north on Church Street, which ends at a staircase. Climb to the top, and you will have a great view of the Mackinac Bridge and the roof of Mission Point Resort, 0.3 mile from the ferry docks. Take the paved road (Huron Road) east about 100

yards, and the trailhead for Manitou Trail will be on your right.

The Manitou Trail squeezes itself between the paved road and the 100-foot-high escarpment. Hugging the crag, take a gander of the view downward onto the masses of bikers circumnavigating the island. In reality, that is what you are doing–winding through a cedar forest while making a circle loop. Within 0.7 mile, humanity will return, as you reach Arch Rock, a popular destination on the island. This geological formation was sculpted by the workings of Lake Huron's wave action back when the lake levels were much higher. There are bathrooms, overlooks, and a picnic area.

Continuing, take the staircase up to the Nicolet Watch Tower, a memorial to Jean Nicolet, the first European to pass through this area, by canoe, in 1634. Split off to the north just past the overlook, and the pathway's name changes to Tranquil Bluff Trail. Amble along, hugging the high, steep banks of the bluff, formed by the ancient Lake Algonquin. It is important to note that if you bring children on these trails, there are many opportunities for them to tumble down the steep banks, so walk carefully between the children and the drop-off, and hold onto them.

The Tranquil Bluff Trail will come to Leslie Road a couple of times. Keep your eyes peeled when it goes back into the woods, as the turns are not marked. At the 2-mile point in your walk, the Murray Trail will come in from your right, then Soldier's Garden Trail at 2.1 miles. Tranquil Bluff Trail turns inland at this point and becomes safe for everyone.

Cross Scott's Road at 2.5 miles, and your course becomes flat and wide, and you will pick up speed. Within 1,000 feet, you will take a left onto Swamp Trail, which is not swampy at all—it just ends at a swamp after you have hiked downhill, passing an intersection with the Porter Hank Trail at 3.2 miles and reaching British Landing Road at 3.5 miles. Keep your eyes open for the rare yellow lady's slipper orchids in this area. Take the paved road north about 100 feet and progress back onto British Landing Trail and into the woods. British Landing Trail is narrow and winding, and although bikes and horses are allowed on this and all other trails, it is very unlikely that you will see one here.

Continue downhill on British Landing Trail, and you will reach an observation platform at 3.9 miles. Take the stairs to the bottom, and follow the interpretive trail 0.1 mile to the British Landing Nature Center. A small and modest center, it has bathrooms, drinking water, and a phone. The best part is that it is across from the Cannonball Drive Inn, which serves hot food and cold drinks. Of course it's not really a drive-in—remember that automobiles are banned from the island—but you can walk up to place your order for some pasties and other fare.

From this point, there is no direct route using a hiking trail to get back to the ferry docks. There are a couple of golf courses and, of all things, an airport in the way. Just take M 185 counterclockwise 3.4 miles back to town, enjoying the view of the Straits of Mackinac, Lake Huron wildlife, and the culture that tourists and residents bring to the island. You'll pass the Grand Hotel along the way.

32

Park Hiking Trail

Place: Muskallonge Lake State Park

Total distance: 2 miles

Hiking time: 45 minutes to one hour

Gradient: Easy

High points: Forested dunes, access to Lake Superior

Maps: USGS 7.5' Muskallonge Lake West; Muskallonge Lake State Park map; maps at trail intersections

Amenities: Modern campground, and a small convenience store at each end of the park

Footwear: Tennis shoes

Pets: Yes

SUMMARY

A great leg stretcher, this is a loop trail primarily used by day users and campers. Although it flanks Lake Superior and Muskallonge Lake, the trail never comes into direct contact with either, although it comes very close.

Most of the trail is covered with wood chips, and your hike is nearly flat, with a few short climbs (one moderately difficult), and a long but very gradual ascent. You'll parallel the two lakes, and there are social trails that can bring you to either. The North Country Trail also uses part of this loop along the Lake Superior shore.

This area is the former site of Deer Park, a lumbering town in the late 1800s. Before the logging boom, it was an encampment for Native Americans. Millions of board feet of white pine were processed here, floating in Muskallonge Lake, awaiting their turn at the sawmill. As with nearly all forestry operations in the late 1800s, after the logs were removed, the settlement became a ghost town, and all that remains of its lumbering past are some pilings and submerged logs in the lake.

ACCESS

From Grand Marais, take H-58 east for 5 miles. H-58 will parallel Lake Superior then turn south, changing name to County Route 433 (but locally called H 58 as well). At 0.4 mile after it turns south, turn left (east) onto CR 407. Park at the Muskallonge State Park picnic area.

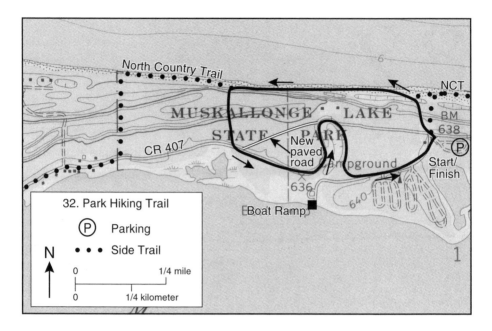

From the picnic area, walk to the contact area, then turn north on the entrance drive and cross the paved road. Take the path less traveled, avoiding the obvious board-walk staircase and instead veering left toward the trailhead, which has a numbered post and a map. It is to the left of a sign summarizing the history of Chief Kawgayoshday, who lived in the area.

THE TRAIL

Mostly disregarded by sunbathers and other beach users, this amble is for trekkers not wishing to get sand between their toes or in their shoes. The trail goes through a mixed forest of balsam fir, sugar maple, and boreal striped maple.

At the 0.2-mile mark, you reach the first numbered post (#2) with a map. Walk into the woods and come to a Y-intersection in 100 yards. Hang a right, and go downhill to the next numbered post (#3). Turn left, go through an open spot in the canopy, and

continue straight ahead. You'll have to push back some undergrowth obscuring the trail on the ground. There are no trail markers at this point, but the way is obvious once you reenter the forest, as your course is wide, duff-covered, and straight as you go uphill.

Quite spongy and lumpy to start, your footing quickly becomes sandy and flat. Lake Superior is immediately on your right, down a sandy and shrub-covered slope. There are several social trails, and at any time in this area, you can go down to the beach. Do this now, because the terrain will gradually head uphill from this point on, and you will find yourself unable to access the beach safely.

Parallel an old sand ridge on the left that has some American yew growing on it. There are also a large number of striped maples, small trees seldom growing more than 30 feet high. Look for the striped maple's characteristic green- and white-striped bark. Very shade-tolerant, this tree is

Lake Superior Beach viewed from trail

slow-growing and short-lived. It is a favorite food for deer and moose.

Carry on uphill, and at the 0.5-mile mark is a North Country Trail (NCT) sign behind the park headquarters. Walk between the building and the forest, and head back into the woods, continuing your slow climb. The trail is very wide, and the woodland floor gives way to starflower, Canada mayflower, small white spruces, and bunchberry. There is the occasional blueberry bush that will gladly give up its fruits for your pleasure in late summer, provided the resident wildlife has not beaten you to it.

Trail markers become evident at this point—you'll see both Department of Natural Resources (DNR) trailway and NCT blue painted rectangular blazes for the next 0.3 mile. At the 0.7-mile mark, looking to the right, you will be about 50 feet above the beach. Massive white pines line the way, and some have had the misfortune to fall down the sandy banks to the beach. Lake Superior ice usually builds up along these shores, protecting the forested dunes and high banks. With some recent warmer-than-normal winters and record low water levels, the ice just has not built up, and the banks have lost trees that had grown here for more than a hundred years. Park staff keep the trail clear of these massive beasts, and you can spend time counting growth rings on some of the victims of our recent mild winters and low water levels.

At 0.8 mile you'll find signpost #4 and more large white pines. Turn left into the woods and come to the top of a long and sandy ridge. Large hemlocks dominate here, and you will head downhill, losing some of the elevation you had gained. Continuing straight will take you west on the North Country Trail. If you were so inclined, you could make a day of it by pacing yourself 7.5 miles to the Blind Sucker Pathway and making a lollipop loop of nearly 20 miles.

Park Hiking Trail

Walk south through more northern hardwood forest toward the paved road. Your footing becomes loose with sand, but the trail remains wide as it reaches post #5 and the road. Cross the road, and from here to the end the path will be wide and covered with wood chips. A few hundred feet after crossing the road, you will reach the 1-mile mark and leave the woods, walking through mostly open habitat with grasses and sparse trees, including balsam poplar.

A boreal species that reaches its southern limit in the Upper Peninsula, balsam poplar is not easily identified, since in shape and appearance it resembles our regular and very common poplar. You can identify the leaves by their balsam fragrance and their oily feel on young trees. Pinching a bud or leaf stem may emit a sticky substance, similar to popping a pustule on a balsam fir.

At 1.3 miles, the trail parallels a dried-up bay that was in all likelihood connected to Muskallonge Lake. You can see the boat launch and campground across this depression. At 1.5 miles, return to the paved road and squeeze between it and the bay, continuing to parallel it, and then reenter the woods, coming to the campground drive.

At post #6, turn left and follow the campground entrance drive, walking by the sanitation station at 1.8 miles and ending at your parking area at 2 miles.

33

North Country Trail: Deer Park to Mouth of Two Hearted River

Place: Lake Superior State Forest

Total distance: 12.9 miles

Hiking time: 1–2 days

Gradient: Mostly flat with some moderate climbs

Highpoints: Lake Superior Shore, dunes

Maps: USGS 7.5' Muskallonge Lake East, Betsy Lake NW; NCT MI-09

Amenities: Deer Park has a convenience store. At the mouth of the Two Hearted River is an outfitter (Rainbow Lodge) with a landing strip.

Footwear: Hiking boots

Pets: Yes

SUMMARY

It is amazing that one of the most incredible beach walking experiences in the UP is so lightly used. Once the North Country Trail leaves Pictured Rocks, it is as if aliens beamed up all the beleaguered backpackers to the mother ship. Your mission, if you choose to accept it, will be likely devoid of other hikers.

Deer Park was a major locale for the market hunting of white-tailed deer in the 1800s. Essentially wiped out, deer populations did not return to any huntable levels for many years. Deer Park has a small store, where you can also rent cabins. The mouth of the Two Hearted River is home to a state forest campground and Rainbow Lodge, a full-service outfitter offering camping, hotel, guide services, car spotting, and even a small airport.

The North Country Trail (NCT) parallels the beach on the low foredunes within a stone's throw of the lake. Unfortunately, two factors—one natural and one manmade—have altered the trail's location. Recent low water levels and little to no ice formation on Lake Superior have led to severe erosion of the beach and trail. Combine this with some private inholdings, and the marked NCT jogs in and out from the beach numerous times. However, a recent Michigan Supreme Court ruling allows citizens a right-of-way on our Great Lakes beaches between the water's edge and the high-water mark. You cannot camp, sunbathe, or otherwise linger in this zone, but it is legal to traverse it.

Mouth of the Two Hearted River

Since this is the North Country Trail, the local NCT chapter is responsible for its maintenance and upkeep. Take comfort in the fact that, although remote, the trail here is in relatively good shape. As elsewhere, the trail is marked with blue rectangular blazes and NCT logos—use these as your guide on your hike.

However, because the path on the ground may be nonexistent at times and there may be no landmarks, having a GPS unit to pinpoint your location is recommended. It is very easy to lose your way and difficult to ascertain exactly where you are.

Otherwise, enjoy an amazing walk using the beach, admire the dunes, and listen to Gitche Gumee play nature's music.

ACCESS

West trailhead: From Grand Marais, take H-58 east 5 miles. H-58 will parallel Lake Superior then turn south, changing its name

to CR 433. At 0.4 mile after it turns south, turn left (east) onto CR 407. Park at Muskallonge Lake State Park. Walk down CR 407 about 1 mile, and the trailhead will be on the north side of the road. Enquire at the various businesses in Deer Park for local parking.

East trailhead: From Paradise, take M 123 through Tahquamenon Falls State Park. Four miles past the entrance to Upper Falls, turn right (north) onto CR 500. After 7 miles, turn left (west) onto CR 414, go 4 miles, and turn right (north) onto CR 423. CR 423 ends at the Two Hearted River State Forest Campground, after passing Rainbow Lodge. Access the North Country Trail at the footbridge over the river.

THE TRAIL

When in doubt, stick to the beach.

With that sage piece of advice, follow the blue blazes toward Lake Superior from

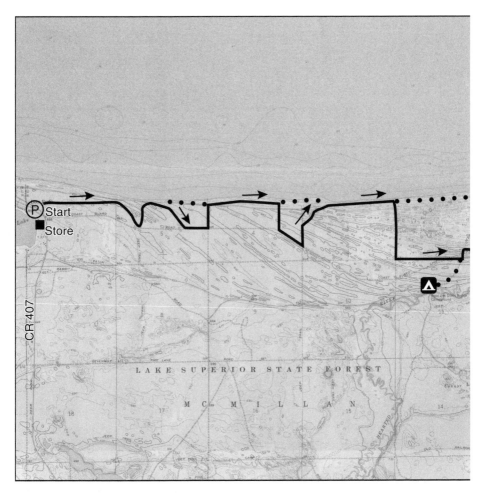

Deer Park. Traipse through the forest 0.4 mile up on a low, forested bluff. Pay close attention to the trail and the markers, as there are no real landmarks like road signs, streams, manufactured structures, or the like on your entire trip.

At the 1-mile mark, you'll negotiate your first private inholding, jutting 0.3 mile inland, hopping onto Coast Guard Line Road for 0.1 mile, then head back to the left (north) 0.3 mile to the beach, only to walk another 0.4 mile, then angle southeast 0.4 mile to Coast Guard Line Road. Keep your eyes open, as you'll go off road, back to the north, in another 0.4 mile. Hike due north

0.2 mile back to the lake, and turn right (east).

You can choose to walk Coast Guard Line Road until it ends at Lake Superior, about 1.5 miles from the mouth of the Two Hearted River. If you choose this route, you will be sandwiched between the lake and the river. If you choose the trail and end up lost, take a bearing north to the lake or south to the river.

Continue along the lakeside 0.7 mile and venture inland again, back to Coast Guard Line Road, 0.2 mile, then angle left (southeast) on Old Coast Guard Road 0.3 mile and come to an intersection with a fire lane.

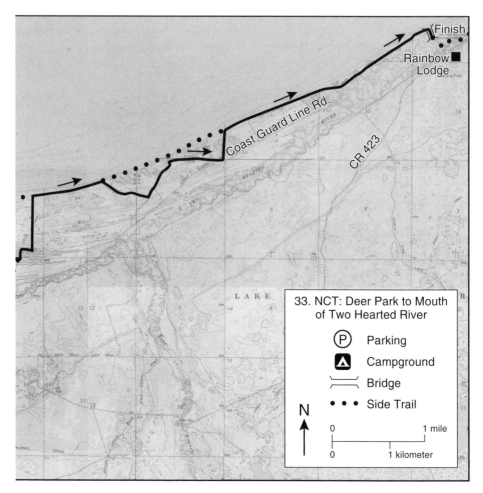

33. NCT: Deer Park to Mouth of Two Hearted River

P   Parking

▲   Campground

Bridge

• • •   Side Trail

N

0   1 mile

0   1 kilometer

Take this lane north, and 0.3 mile later, the road splits in two. Take the path to the (northeast), and hike almost 0.6 mile back to Lake Superior.

This stretch of trail parallels the shore for 0.7 mile before taking a 90-degree turn to the right (south) 0.5 mile back to a two-track. Turn left (east), walk 0.6 mile, and Coast Guard Line Road will come in from your right. Veer left, walk along the road, and the trailhead back to the lake is 0.2 mile farther. On your right, look for a two-track coming in from the south. This leads to Reed and Green Bridge State Forest Campground, an alternative starting point.

Starting at Reed and Green Bridge may make for a less complex hike, as the two-track that leaves the campground to the north makes a straight shot for the lake and joins up with the North Country Trail.

It is 0.5 mile from Coast Guard Line Road to Lake Superior. When you reach the shore, turn right (east), and the trail hugs the shore for 0.7 mile, then veers inland, winding 2 miles through the forested dunes using fire lanes and trail, even coming back briefly to Coast Guard Line Road.

Once you reach Lake Superior, experience an uninterrupted slog through sandy footing for 3.1 miles until you reach the

                             Land of Hiawatha

mouth of the Two Hearted River and the state forest campground. Cross the suspension bridge into the busy campground and share your story about the zigzag meander you accomplished, hopefully without losing your way or your mind.

34

Scott Point

Place: Gould City Township Park

Total distance: 1.5 miles

Hiking time: 1 hour

Gradient: Flat

High points: Piping plovers, cobble beach, dunes, Lake Huron iris, remote location

Maps: USGS 7.5' Point Patterson

Amenities: Picnic area

Footwear: Tennis shoes

Pets: Not recommended

SUMMARY

Saved by the Michigan Chapter of the Nature Conservancy, Scott Point juts into the northern reaches of Lake Michigan. This small spit of land has historically been a seasonal nesting ground for the endangered piping plover, but other rare plants and animals also make their homes in the sand and cobble. Gould City Township Park, a modest park with swing sets and picnic tables, is your launching-off point.

In the past, the thoroughfare ended at the beach and provided access to off-road vehicles. Unfortunately, irresponsible users damaged the habitats and terrorized the wildlife for years, causing nearly irreparable harm. After acquiring the land, the Nature Conservancy turned it over to the Lake Superior State Forest for management. Off-road vehicles have since been banned, although there are still a few scofflaws who disobey the signs and barriers. Be aware of this when exploring the beach.

ACCESS

From St. Ignace, take US 2 west. Six miles past the M 117 intersection, Gould City and the road named after it head south toward Lake Michigan. Take Gould City Road south, through Gould City (more of a small village) 10 miles until it ends at the lake.

THE TRAIL

This is more an exploration than a trek down a marked and maintained corridor. There are a mishmash of game trails, old two-tracks,

Land of Hiawatha

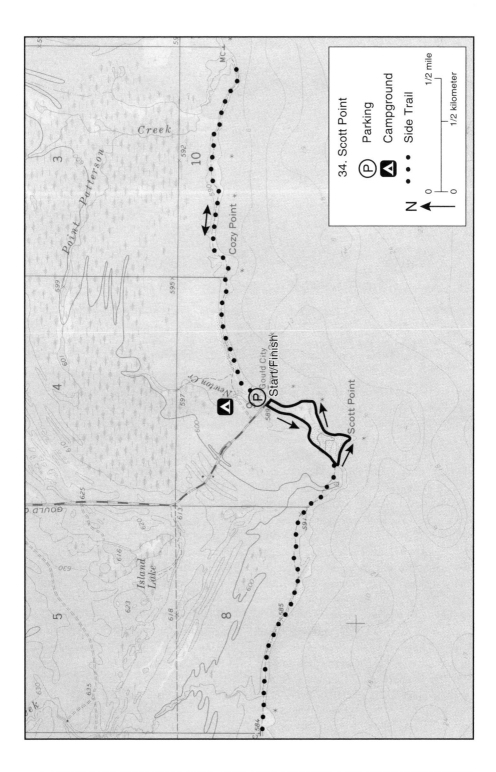

Boulders are strewn about at Scott Point

and social trails to explore or get hopelessly lost. From the parking area, cross the paved Gould City Road and maneuver around the closed gate onto an abandoned two-track. You will be surrounded by 30-foot cedars on both sides while striding along past a carpet of mosses and Lake Huron irises. This diminutive relative of the garden-variety iris is a federally listed endangered species. Growing only in calcareous (mineral-rich) soils, the Lake Huron iris is strictly limited to the immediate shorelines of the northern Great Lakes. These flowers bloom from mid-July to mid-August, making an explosion of color in an otherwise shady forest.

Take the two-track east, and after about 0.4 mile, the cedars will disappear altogether on your right and thin out on your left. The two-track bends around a bit and starts to peter out. In another 0.1 mile, when your confidence may be waning and you see what amounts to a game trail up the backside of a sand dune, it is time to get a little adventurous.

There is just enough sand and strength in the prevailing winds to create these modest sand dunes. It is interesting to note that about one-third of the plants you find in a Great Lakes sand dune are also found growing in similar habitats on the Atlantic coast.

While on the dune, admire the beach grasses holding the loosely gathered sand. Calamovilfa is especially powerful in binding sand to make it more stable for other plants to take root in subsequent years. Balsam poplar and jackpine account for the bulk of the trees away from the beach. Sand dunes are quite rare in the Upper Peninsula, and although this one is quite small compared to, say, Grand Sable Dune, take the time to enjoy it.

This is a prime example of why a compass is one of the 10 essentials. Simply take a southward bearing and you will go up and

Land of Hiawatha

over a low dune, through a thin smattering of poplars and jackpines, and find yourself on a cobble beach in about 0.25 mile.

If you have the time and desire, take a beach walk west to Birch Point, 2.5 miles away. Alternatively, take the beach back to the west, following the shore. Notice the abundance of not only the cobble, but also massive glacial erratics, some the size of small cars. When you reach the actual point, the forest comes out toward the tip. On the west side of the point is an intermittent wetland that can be traversed one of two ways. Looking west, you can see the park, picnic area, and probably your car.

During low water, you can hopscotch across the cobbles back to the dry beach, and you will be mere 200 yards from your car. During high water, follow the semicircular sand beach inland that makes a lip between the cobble beach and the large wetland behind it.

This particular wetland, an interdunal wetland, is at the mercy of fluctuating water levels, plant succession, and the movement of sand. Uncommon habitats, interdunal wetlands have incredible plant diversity. You will have to push through the barrier of cedars and tamaracks to enjoy the nonflowering plants such as panic grasses, bulrushes, beak-rushes, horsetails, and sedges. Although they may not be visually appealing, they are important to many animals for food.

Flowering plants include smaller fringed gentian, small-flowered gerardia, and lobelias, along with two uncommon goldenrods—Houghton's and Ohio. This may appear like a stable habitat, but all it takes is a natural event like a storm or rising water levels to wash away the barrier between Lake Michigan and the wetland to eliminate this interesting habitat. The trees are the first line of defense, keeping the ice in the lake and preventing it from scraping away what little soil is found here. Take your opportunity now to witness this area: geologically speaking, it will be gone very soon!

Continue your hike along the beach as long as you feel comfortable walking. Within 2 miles of Scott Point, there are two more points to the west: Cozy Point 0.7 mile from the park and Point Patterson 1.1 miles west of Cozy Point. When you have had enough of the Lake Michigan beach, just turn around and head back.

35

Pine Ridge Nature Trail

Place: Seney National Wildlife Refuge

Total distance: 1.4 miles

Hiking time: ¾−1 hour

Gradient: Flat

High points: Abundant and diverse birds, otters, black bears, beavers

Maps: USGS 7.5' Seney

Amenities: Visitor center, interpretive trail signs

Footwear: Tennis shoes

Pets: Yes.

SUMMARY

Under most circumstances, unscrupulous land speculators, poor logging methods, and failed agricultural practices would not benefit wildlife. Of course, if you were the designer for the Seney National Wildlife Refuge, you would plan to do quite the opposite.

Seney's history began in the late 1800s when lumber barons stripped the Upper Peninsula of its magnificent forests. The land was left barren, and fires were deliberately set to burn off the remaining deadfalls in preparation for farming.

Lured to the eastern UP with promises of rich, organic soils, farmers could only dream of making a good living off the land. The swamps were drained and so were the farmers, as it was nearly impossible to raise any sort of productive crop. One by one, farms were claimed by the government for back taxes.

In 1934, the federal government brought in the Civilian Conservation Corps. The CCC workers toiled in the mosquito-infested wetlands building dikes and ponds, impounding more than 7,000 acres of water in temporary pools.

Rising from the ashes, Seney National Wildlife Refuge today is a premier sanctuary for wildlife of all kinds. On a trip to the UP, you can pack in an incredible amount of wildlife viewing in as little as a half a day.

Ice still floats in the many ponds as Canada geese arrive around the first day of spring. Chilly and downright inhospitable,

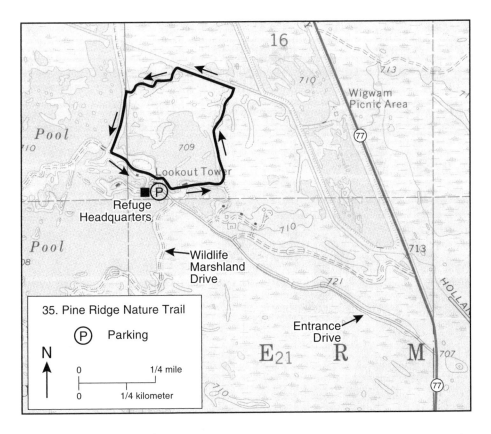

the weather does not deter the other early migrants. Sandhill cranes and red-winged blackbirds are soon to follow, and it's still over a month until the visitor center opens for the season!

Seney is probably the best place in the UP to view such sought-after icons of the wild as the bald eagle, osprey, and the common loon. Scan the treetops for our American symbol and the osprey. Loons are usually seen floating, then diving underwater seeking out a fishy meal.

Late May and early June is the peak time to view birds migrating northward. In the fall, visit at the end of September and early October as they make their way south.

Sometimes, you can make wildlife viewing as hard or as easy as you would like.

From slogging through waist-deep water in a wilderness to viewing wildlife from the comfort of your car, you have several ways to find wildlife at Seney National Wildlife Refuge. The challenge is finding which method of viewing wildlife suits you best.

By far the most popular, the 7-mile wildlife drive allows you to keep your feet dry and quickly traverse the area. Using your car as a blind, scan the numerous marshes and ponds for scores of waterfowl. Grebes, loons, black ducks, and wading herons call the 95,000-acre refuge home.

There are several observation decks, and plenty of places to park your car for close-up looks of wildlife. Keep your ears open and turn off the car occasionally to listen for birds that are often heard, but seldom seen.

Boardwalk on the Pine Ridge Nature Trail

American bitterns make a gulping sound, and common snipes fly overhead, taunting you with a laughing sound, as if they are mocking you.

By foot, stroll the 1.5-mile Pine Ridge Nature Trail in search of signs of bears, swimming otters, and of course singing birds. Take time to smell the flowers, or at least identify them, as you walk through some of the wetter areas. There are several benches where you can rest and boardwalks to keep your feet dry as you enjoy your walk.

Canoeing the Manistique River, either on your own or by hiring an outfitter, allows wildlife viewing that few of the 100,000 annual visitors to Seney get to experience. No boats of any kind are allowed on any of the impoundments. Although it is tempting to float the Driggs River through the 25,000-acre wilderness area, officials recommend sticking to the wider Manistique River. Contact Big Cedar Campground and

Canoe Livery at 906-586-6684; or North-land Outfitters at 1-800-808-3386, or at northoutfitters.com.

This circular trail starts and ends at the visitor center. It is flat and traverses some sandy wooded ridges and takes you alongside wetlands and ponds. There are several boardwalks and many wildlife viewing opportunities.

ACCESS

From Seney, take M 77 south 10 miles, and turn right into the wildlife refuge. Park at the visitor center, which will be on the right. The trail starts immediately to the left of the visitor center.

THE TRAIL

Park at the visitor center, and after viewing the exhibits, turn left as you exit and follow the nature trail sign. Head east on a mowed grass path between two manmade ponds that are filled with assorted wild residents of the feathered, furry, fishy, scaly, and slimy variety. Almost immediately, you're greeted by a trail map. Cross a small footbridge whose underpinnings are clogged with debris courtesy of the local beavers. Look for lodges along the shores of the ponds to confirm their presence. Even if you see no lodge, the woody vegetation with characteristic chew marks will give them away.

At 0.2 mile, you reach a trail intersection with a DO NOT ENTER sign on the trail going to the right. Turn left and head north along another berm bordered on the left by the pond and on the right by an expansive emergent marsh. This is a great place to listen for the throaty *glump-GLUMP* of an American bittern. Mostly heard and rarely seen, this heron relative has cryptic coloration, but a distinctive call.

The grass path continues for another 0.2 mile and rises gently and winds northeast through a grove of jackpines for another 0.1 mile. The trail remains wide, and though there are no trail markers, they really aren't necessary. A side trail comes in from the right and intersects your trail.

Descend slightly through this patch of forest dominated mostly by maturing red pine, turning right onto a boardwalk that enters a shrub swamp, which gives way to marsh on both sides of your trail. This floating boardwalk merely sits on the ground keeping your footing dry as you make a beeline in a west-northwest direction. At 0.8 mile, the boardwalk starts bending to the left, crosses a bridge, and you'll be back on a sandy ridge forested with red pines and jackpines.

Up to this point, your interpretive graphics have been small and simple, with basic information about the natural history of the area. Greeting you in the woods is a large panel graphic highlighting the plight of neotropical migrating birds. Because Seney is mostly known for its waterfowl and birds of prey, the colorful warblers living in the area take most birders by surprise. With such varied habitats, nearly 30 species can be found at some time of the year at Seney.

Continue walking on a ridge through the thin forest, and at 0.9 mile, you'll come to a two-track gravel road. Turn left, following the trail signs, and in 75 yards, veer left onto a grass trail, avoiding walking up the driveway of a private residence. Cross a small footbridge, again clogged by beaver activity, and walk up to the refuge headquarters. Walk toward the flagpole, and you can see the visitor center and the parking area to your left. Pass by the lookout tower, stay on the pavement, and return to your vehicle.

36

Falls Trail
(Upper to Lower Falls)

Place: Tahquamenon Falls State Park

Total distance: 4.3 miles (one way)

Hiking time: 2½–4 hours (one way)

Gradient: Easy to moderate

High points: Two major waterfalls, wild river walk, old-growth forest

Maps: USGS 7.5' Betsy Lake South, Timberlost; Tahquamenon Falls State Park map; NCT MI-09

Amenities: Modern campgrounds, restaurants, gift shops, interpretive stations

Footwear: Hiking boots

Pets: Yes

SUMMARY

This segment of the North Country Trail is probably the most heavily used segment of this 4,600-mile long National Scenic Trail. The Falls Trail is a popular day hike, attracting tens of thousands visitors annually.

At both ends of the trail are Michigan's showpiece waterfalls, Upper Tahquamenon and Lower Tahquamenon Falls. East of the Mississippi River, Upper Tahquamenon Falls is second only to Niagara Falls in volume. At peak flow, more than 50,000 gallons of water per second rushes over its 50-foot-high, 200-foot wide precipice. Lower Tahquamenon Falls are a series of falls and rapids flowing around an island, over a quarter-mile stretch.

The passageway for the first mile from each falls is mostly inland and up in elevation. The middle 2 miles navigates mostly along the edge of the river. This is a wild area with regular sightings of bald eagles, river otters, beavers, and white-tailed deer.

The Tahquamenon River meanders nearly 100 miles, draining nearly 800 square miles of mostly swampland, including the Great Manistique Swamp. The copper color comes from tannins leached by decomposing mosses, spruces, tamaracks, and cedars. Tannins are the same chemicals that gives your tea its color.

This is the land of Henry Wadsworth Longfellow's 1855 epic poem *The Song of Hiawatha*—"by the rushing Tahquamenaw"—where Hiawatha built his canoe. The Ojibwa Native Americans harvested fish and other animals here for centuries before the lumber

Land of Hiawatha

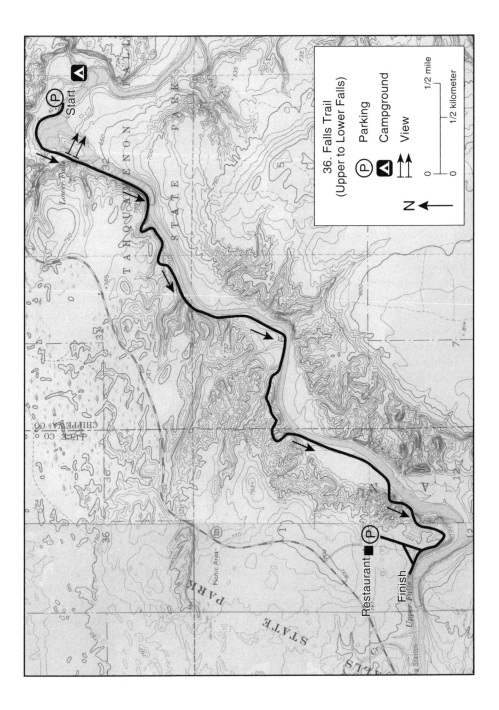

36. Falls Trail
(Upper to Lower Falls)

ⓟ Parking
🅰 Campground
⬆⬆ View

0   1/2 kilometer
0   1/2 mile

N ←

barons arrived on the scene in the 19th century and harvested logs by the millions, processing them in local mills. However, many old-growth groves in the area were inadvertently spared because the steepness of the slopes made them inaccessible to that era's logging methods.

This is an out-and-back trail, although on some occasions a shuttle may be available. Check with park officials before embarking.

ACCESS

Both falls are located on M 123 between Newberry and Paradise. Paradise is closer, only 10 miles from Lower Falls and 14 from Upper Falls. Newberry is 21 miles from Upper Falls.

The Lower Falls trailhead is 0.8 mile past the contact station, past both campgrounds. There is ample paved parking. Take the paved walkway and stay to the left, walking past the concession area.

For the Upper Falls trailhead, parking is available immediately past the contact station. Take the paved path and stay to the left. The trailhead is located at the top of the stairs leading down into the gorge.

THE TRAIL

Rugged, and root- and rock-infested, the Falls Trail will take the average person a little longer to hike than might be expected, not only because of the trail conditions, but also due to taking extra time to observe the sheer natural beauty of the area.

From the parking area at Lower Falls, take the paved path, then the boardwalk 0.4 mile through maturing forest to the first overlook at the largest cascade at the falls. The boardwalk continues past two more overlooks and peters out at a sign that reads UPPER FALLS 4 MILES, 8 MILES ROUND TRIP. Gaze beyond and you will see why the timid and inexperienced hiker may forgo the

seemingly short river corridor. Roots, rocks, deep shade, and muddy underfooting are what immediately greet the hiker. This is because many of the half million yearly visitors cautiously explore this area, wearing down the soil and exposing roots and rocks.

About 0.2 mile after the end of the boardwalk is a small sign indicating that the way to the Upper Falls proceeds to the right, keeping you from getting lost on the many social trails in the area. The roar of the cascading falls in the background is softened as you walk up the stairs into what was a canopy of mature beeches and sugar maples. That is, until the beech bark disease was introduced into the park a few years ago, probably by a careless camper transporting infected firewood. Michigan DNR staff removed many of the stately, old-growth beech trees, opening up the canopy. The climb is near 100 feet, and the trail winds around the upland area and at 0.7 mile, starts descending toward the river using the edge of an escarpment.

Although you are on the North Country Trail, there are no NCT emblems or blazes, just the traditional painted blue dot placed by park staff. The ground is covered in Canada mayflower, club moss, sarsaparilla, and emerging maples.

The trail is very wide and well worn, with the occasional well-placed footbridge to cross gullies and the numerous springs in the area. Continue with a moderate downhill walk, crossing the contour of the embankment to your right and seeing the river through the forest on your left. You will reach a point about 20 feet above the river and carry on moving through the mature hemlock, beech, and maple forest. You cannot physically reach the river unless you want to slide down on your behind and go feet-first into the copper-colored waters of the Tahquamenon.

Upper Tahquamenon Falls

At 1 mile (there is a post) you'll finally come to the edge of the river and lose the roots and rocks. You will wind in and out of the forest for the next 2 miles, following the river. Keep on the lookout for otter slides, which are matted-down grass pathways perpendicular to the river.

At 1.5 miles is a staircase to negotiate around a place where the trail has eroded away. Look for a large patch of ostrich fern about 0.2 mile past the downhill staircase. When not in the woods, progress through some brushy areas consisting of raspberry plants, alder, and young birch.

At 2 miles, you are still on flat terrain and hugging the river. There is a two-sided bench for a quick break. If you are doing an out-and-back, you are only one-quarter of the way! The trail is mostly packed sand with few roots and no rocks between the 1- and 3-mile markers.

At the 2.5-mile mark, a set of staircases will take you up away from the river onto a ridge, with a 100-foot elevation gain and a bench at the top, 0.2 mile from the start of your climb.

Wind through a sugar maple forest, turning toward the river, and then an escarpment. Descend a 71-step stairway down to the river's edge. Parallel the river through beeches, maples, and sugar maples as you reach the 3-mile mark.

Cross a small footbridge, trek through a field of ostrich fern, and come to a short stretch of roots to reach another staircase climb at the 3.3-mile mark. Scale the 54 steps up, then experience some more rooty trail leading to the edge of an escarpment with some steps and roots. After your 100-foot elevation gain, you will be in mature northern hardwood forest again, with old-growth sugar maples and some beeches.

Although you are less than a mile from Upper Falls, it is the roar of traffic on M 123 that you hear through the forest. At the

3.5-mile mark, navigate down, then up and through a ravine back onto level ground. The forest walk winds through sugar maples up on the Niagaran Formation, the same formation that the Tahquamenon flows over to make the Upper Falls. Just 0.3 mile farther along, you will leave the duff-covered path and find yourself at an asphalt pathway. Take the gorge staircase down immediately on your left, or continue straight to view the falls from several overlooks. Although you may have seen only a handful of other hikers during your trip, you will be surrounded by your fellow humans at this very popular tourist attraction. Retrace your steps to return to your car.

37

Whitefish Point

Place: Whitefish Point Bird Observatory

Total distance: 1 mile

Hiking time: 1 hour

Gradient: Flat

High points: Globally Important Bird Area, Lake Superior beach, Great Lakes Shipwreck Museum

Maps: USGS 7.5' Whitefish Point; Whitefish Bird Observatory map

Amenities: Museum has bathrooms and drinking water

Footwear: Flip-flops

Pets: Not recommended and prohibited during bird migration and breeding seasons

SUMMARY

A short drive north of Paradise, Whitefish Point is a popular destination for bird watchers from around the world. Some days, it seems there are more birders than birds on this spit of land jutting into Lake Superior.

This peninsula is a launching point for birds migrating north into Canada. Thousands of sharp-shinned hawks, loons, warblers, and a host of other birds make the trip across the lake into Ontario.

Whitefish Point Bird Observatory, the on-site nature center, is staffed with knowledgeable birders. They are glad to help identify birds and even tell you where some notable birds may be seen in the area.

If you are a serious bird watcher looking to add to your life list, request the Checklist to the Birds of the Whitefish Point Bird Observatory. This guide documents each species and when each is found at the point. This is one of the top 10 bird-watching destinations in North America, so if you aren't a birder already, you may become one.

Even in the middle of summer, be prepared for brisk winds, cool temperatures, and ice-cold Lake Superior water at Whitefish Point.

ACCESS

From the Mackinaw Bridge, continue driving on I-75 north about 5 miles and take the M 123 exit. M 123 goes only west, through Trout Lake, Eckerman, and into Paradise. This state highway will turn west, but you will continue north on Whitefish Point Road until it ends at the parking lot.

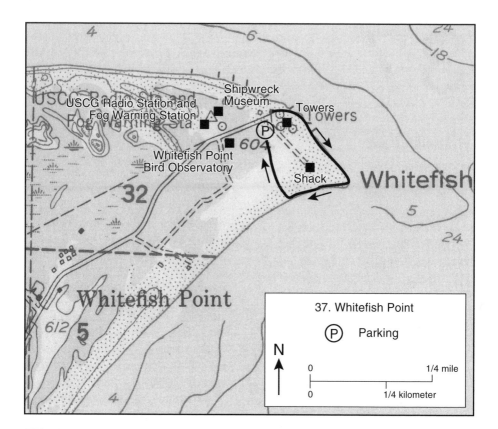

Ⓟ Parking

N

| 0 | | 1/4 mile |
| 0 | | 1/4 kilometer |

THE TRAIL

This is more of a controlled amble using landmarks than a strict trail on a marked path. Once you park, you will notice the Whitefish Point Bird Observatory on the right side of the parking lot, and the lighthouse and Great Lakes Shipwreck Museum on the left side. Park, and head toward the lighthouse across the parking lot, then use the sidewalk. Once you are at the base of the lighthouse and the historical marker, note the boardwalk heading to the right. Take this wide walk toward Lake Superior.

On a clear, calm, sunny day, you will see many visitors walking the beach. Some of them may even be brave enough to venture into the cold waters of Lake Superior. In most years, the lake does not stay above 45

degrees for long. So do not pack the swimming trunks expecting a cool dip. The weather here is highly variable: you could be wearing winter gear even in midsummer if the wind is whipping off the lake from the north. Fog is very prevalent as well—the point is frequently socked in for days at a time. In winter, ice prevents access to the beach altogether.

From the high point of the boardwalk, scan the horizon for passing freighters. These ships, many much longer than a football field, are most likely carrying iron ore, but sometimes wheat and corn. Whitefish Bay is a designated harbor of refuge during stormy weather. This was not the case when the SS *Edmund Fitzgerald* tried making it around the point in a storm on November 10, 1975.

A passing freighter makes the turn around Whitefish Point

Tragically, the ship went down and 29 lives were lost. The Great Lakes Shipwreck Museum is a testament to shipping, and to the plight of this ore freighter.

Take the boardwalk down 0.1 mile to the white, sandy beach and trudge through the sand to the water's edge. Turn right (east) and follow the beach east 0.3 mile to the tip of the point. Along the way, feel free to beachcomb for rocks and driftwood while soaking up the view. Birders revel in the opportunity to witness migrating owls, hawks, and water birds. There is an excellent checklist available at the Whitefish Bird Observatory office. Over 300 species of birds have been documented since 1978.

Once you reach the tip, take the bend around to the south for a couple of hundred feet. You will notice a small shack sitting about 100 yards from the shore. Start walking toward the shack, and keep to the left of the shack (south). You'll feel cobbles and sand underfoot or between your toes.

A short distance beyond the shack, a bona fide trail begins, which appears to be packed gravel. You will cross another trail within 0.1 mile of the shack, and the ground will become covered with juniper and bearberry. As you continue, you will enter a small forest of stunted jackpines. Keep your eyes open for small songbirds flitting about, especially in the spring and fall. You will see many side trails with what appear to be badminton nets—this is a bird banding area used by research scientists, so please keep out.

Pass the Coast Guard radio and fog warning station at 0.8 mile into your journey, and then you will find yourself at the northeast corner of the parking lot within another 0.1 mile. The Whitefish Point Bird Observatory office and gift shop is on your right.

There is one other boardwalk worth mentioning. When taking a walking tour around the historic buildings, look for a sidewalk that takes off from the northwest corner of the shipwreck museum. Skirt between the museum and a bathroom building before entering an uncommon habitat, called a Great Lakes barren. Climb up this boardwalk for another view of Lake Superior.

38

Maywood History Trail

Place: Little Bay de Noc National Forest Recreation Area

Total distance: 0.6 mile

Hiking time: ½ hour

Gradient: Wheelchair accessible

High points: Wheelchair-accessible, interpretive trail, large trees

Maps: Trailhead map

Amenities: Rustic campgrounds with pit toilets, swimming beach, lake access

Footwear: Flip-flops

Pets: Yes

SUMMARY

Constructed in 1993 after the passage of the Americans With Disabilities Act, the Maywood History Trail is surrounded by massive, 200-year-old white pines, hemlocks, and yellow birches. It was apparently spared the axe and plow, probably because this area was being used as a resort during the great lumber boom in the late 1800s. Excellent interpretive signage tells the story of the relationship between Native Americans and European settlers, and describes the natural history of the area.

ACCESS

From Rapid River, take US 2 west 3 miles, turning south on CR 513. Recreation Area entrance is 6 miles south. This is a US Forest Service fee area, and you can pay at the day use area. After paying the fee, continue down the entrance drive, and turn right at the group campground entrance, which is also signed for the Maywood History Trail.

THE TRAIL

A lollipop loop, the path is wide and made of packed, crushed gravel. A trail map at the trailhead gives a blow-by-blow description of the trail, its route, and accessibility.

Your first interpretive station tells the story about being under a cathedral of old-growth hemlock. Although the forest here is composed of 200-year-old trees, it appears a recent event knocked down some of these giants, creating a hole in the canopy.

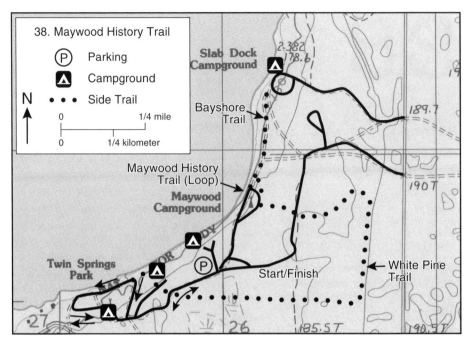

Slab Dock
Campground 🅰

Bayshore
Trail

Maywood History
Trail (Loop)

Maywood
Campground

🅰

Twin Springs
Park

🅰

(P)

Start/Finish

🅰

← White Pine
Trail

Due to the climax forest, the ground cover is very sparse. This makes it easy to scan the forest for fire-damaged trees, as the next graphic points out. Red pines are the best trees to examine for evidence of past forest fires. Look at the base of the tree for a triangular scar that could be a few inches to a few feet in height. As fire moves through the forest, it wraps around to the backside of a tree, burning it. Red pine bark burns quickly and then moves on—therefore, the fire does minimal damage to the tree.

At 0.1 mile, reach the return trail coming from your left. Continue in a counterclockwise direction, cross the White Pine Trail, and come to a sign showing pictures of socialites picnicking under what were then 75-year-old hemlocks! Take a seat and think of days gone by, as there is a bench associated with every graphic.

Not only did families come here to picnic and vacation, large gatherings of social clubs filled the forest on an annual basis during the late 1800s and early 1900s. Thousands of people would descend on this area. One would think the feet of so many people would cause irreparable harm to the forest, but your eyes tell you differently, seeing all the young hemlocks sprouting from the ground.

The Maywood Hotel, built in 1904, was the main attraction, sitting in the woods under stately hemlocks. This was during the great lumber boom, when many people came up from Chicago by train to escape the summer heat by spending time at the hotel. This short-lived resort was abandoned by 1930 and fell into disrepair. Nothing remains of the hotel today, although you can see evidence of the foundations. Look for small, earthen mounds and depressions in the ground. Some cabins were built here as well. The only signs of their existence are that the forest was

The Maywood History Trail is wheelchair accessible

cleared for their use and still has not grown back today.

The Bayshore Trail, paralleling the beach, shares the Maywood History Trail for about 0.1 mile in more open habitat. You will then come out to an overlook on the lake. Here, a springhouse used to provide drinking water for the residents of the hotel. Look below for signs of seepages that are still present today.

Cross the White Pine Trail for a second time and watch as the Bayshore Trail continues straight and the Maywood Trail bends to the left back into the woods. Here is the story of the Native Americans who once lived in the area, known as the "bear clan," or "noquets," a word meaning "bear."

Your only climb for this amble is a small incline that takes you up to an old sand ridge where the beach used to lap up onto the shore thousands of years ago. Complete your lollipop loop and turn right at the intersection to return to the parking area.

IV

Pictured Rocks

39

Au Sable Light Station

Place: Pictured Rocks National Lakeshore

Total distance: 2.4 miles round trip

Hiking time: 2 hours

Gradient: Flat

Highpoints: Lighthouse, shipwrecks, sand beach

Maps: USGS 7.5' Au Sable Point

Amenities: Rustic camping, pit toilets, potable water at trailhead.

Footwear: Tennis shoes

Pets: Yes

SUMMARY

Au Sable Light Station offers a flat walk on a sandy beach rich with history about lighthouses, Great Lakes shipping, and shipwrecks. The trail starts at the end of Hurricane River Campground and parallels Lake Superior for 1.5 miles.

Au Sable Point has been a hazard to shipping since mariners started traversing Lake Superior in the early 1600s. When the canal opened at Sault Ste. Marie in 1855, the increase in shipping brought an increase in ships bottoming out at Au Sable Point. The sandstone formations come within several feet of the surface, which is not so bad, except that these reefs are several thousand feet from the point. Thick fog had a synergistic effect with the reefs, causing an abnormally high number of shipwrecks in the latter part of the 19th century.

Au Sable Light Station went into service on August 19, 1874. Originally, the light burned lard, then kerosene, before having a third-order Fresnel lens installed, making the point visible 18 miles out into Lake Superior.

Various light keepers kept vigil in this 86-foot lighthouse, modeled after the Outer Island Light in the Apostle Islands. Although their first order of duty was to keep the light running, the keepers spent a lot of their time clearing the area around the lighthouse of anything that could burn in case a forest fire— a real threat even today—came near. Keepers made daily journal entries, noting everything from weather events and the number of fish caught to hunting adventures. Many of these

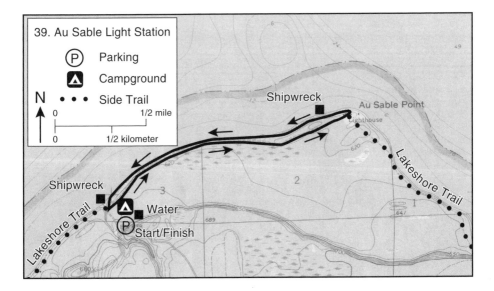

39. Au Sable Light Station

(P) Parking

🔺 Campground

N • • • Side Trail

0   1/2 mile

0   1/2 kilometer

Shipwreck

Au Sable Point

Lighthouse

Lakeshore Trail

Shipwreck

Lakeshore Trail

Water

Start/Finish

stories can be read in the foghorn building, where journal entries are posted.

Today, the various buildings at the light station are being restored. During the summer months, tours are available of the lighthouse, the keeper's quarters, and several outbuildings, including the foghorn building. Plans are to have a museum by 2008.

ACCESS

From Grand Marais, take H 58 12 miles west to Hurricane River Campground. Park

The remains of the Sitka are exposed during low water years

Au Sable Light Station

in the day use area and hike to the east end of the campground loop. Look for a gate and sign indicating the trailhead.

THE TRAIL

Your 2.4-mile out-and-back jaunt is wide, flat, and straight. When you are all through touring and learning the history of the light station, look for a sign on a white building that indicates a staircase to the beach. In years when Lake Superior has low water levels, you will be able to walk right up and explore the remains of two shipwrecks just east of the point.

Although shipwreck and lighthouse history is the focus, note the somewhat boreal feel to your surroundings. Balsam fir, paper birch, red maple, white spruce, and striped maple line the path. Flowers include fireweed and sarsaparilla. It is quite shady and

damp, so you should look for clumps of club moss.

Lake Superior is in full view only a stone's throw away. However, there are only three places you can properly access it on your tour: at the trailhead, at the light station, and a beach access about 1 mile from the trailhead. At the light station, there are many cement paths, and it is best to use them to find your way around, as there is a lot of sensitive vegetation, and ongoing archaeological activities in the area.

The *Sitka* and *Gale Staples* were two very similar ships. Both were double-decked wooden bulk freighters with two masts and were almost identical in length at approximately 275 feet. The remains of both ships are scattered about on the beach and in the shallow waters of Lake Superior. The *Sitka* was loaded with iron ore when it ran aground in October of 1904. Thankfully, the lifesavers at the light station rescued 17 men from the ship.

The beach is sandy, with some sandstone outcroppings. You will come upon the second set of shipwreck remains. The *Gale Staples* was loaded with coal and was driven off course by high winds and grounded on the offshore reef, again in October, but in 1918. Everyone was rescued from the *Gale Staples* as well. There is even a third wreck that occurred here, the *Union,* which sank on September 25, 1873. The remains of this steam barge are out there but have yet to be found.

When you are through exploring, look for a staircase on your left leading back to the campground and parking area.

40

Chapel Falls Loop

Place: Pictured Rocks National Lakeshore

Total distance: 6.7 miles

Hiking time: 3–4 hours

Gradient: Easy

High points: Views of Pictured Rocks, remote beach, waterfall

Maps: USGS 7.5' Pictured Rocks National Lakeshore, Grand Portal Point; NCT MI-10

Amenities: Pit toilets at trailhead, beach. Backcountry campsites at beach.

Footwear: Hiking boots

Pets: Prohibited

SUMMARY

This loop walk circumnavigates Chapel Lake. The terrain is relatively flat, taking you through mature hardwood forests to Lake Superior and unspoiled views of the lake and rock formations.

Wide and well worn, your hike affords you only a few views of Chapel Lake. However, you can get quite close to Chapel Falls and Chapel Rock, and walk Chapel Beach. There is a backcountry campsite for anyone interested in spending the night in this rugged and beautiful area.

Maps, park publications, and park signs disagree on trail distances. These differences are inconsequential to your travels.

ACCESS

From Munising, take H-58 east. About 0.25 mile east of Melstrand, Chapel Road, a gravel and sometimes rough road, takes you north to a parking lot at the trailhead.

THE TRAIL

An interpretive station, trash cans, and pit toilets greet you at the trailhead. This is where modern amenities cease as you stride on the seemingly overused trail northeast through a mostly red maple-dominated forest. Notice the ground cover, which includes Solomon's seal, violets, emerging maple trees, sweet cicely, and trillium. Besides the red maples, other trees include those typical of a northern hardwood forest, including sugar maple, paper birch, and an occasional basswood and white ash.

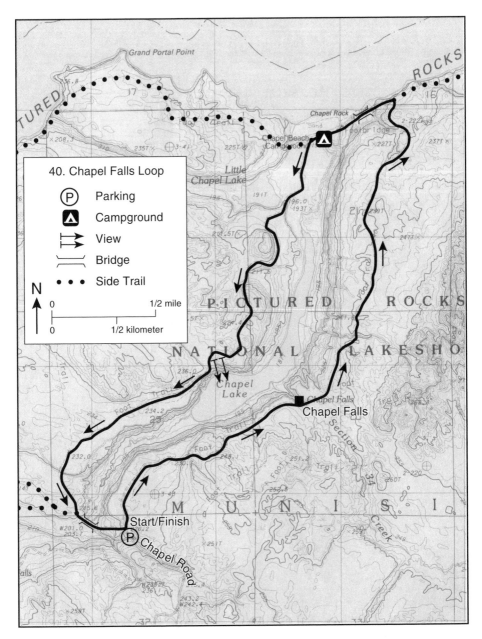

The map legend reads:

40. Chapel Falls Loop

- (P) Parking
- 🔺 Campground
- ⇥ View
- ⊐⊏ Bridge
- • • • Side Trail

N

0 ——————— 1/2 mile

0 ——————— 1/2 kilometer

Grand Portal Point

Chapel Rock

Footbridge

Chapel Beach Campground

Little Chapel Lake

PICTURED ROCKS

NATIONAL LAKESHORE

Chapel Lake

Chapel Falls

MUNISI

Start/Finish

Chapel Road

Although there are no trail markers, you will not need them on this wide and straight trail. Since you are high in elevation, walking just inches above billion-year-old limestone laid down by an ancient sea, the walk is rather flat.

Your first overlook, toward Chapel Lake, is 180 feet from the main trail. Do not get

Chapel Falls

your hopes up—the growing forest has obscured the view that once allowed hikers to take in Chapel Lake in the distance. However, there are some interesting rock formations below the overlook.

The terrain undulates slightly as you continue through the forest. Keep your eyes open for ninebark, an uncommon plant found occasionally in northern forests. Ninebark resembles a small shrub, with compound leaves and tough stems. Its white, compound flower resembles a small ball of popcorn.

You'll also start to see other species of trees, such as balsam fir and northern hemlock. Because Lake Superior is so close, moisture from the mighty lake influences the local climate, giving the area a more boreal aspect than it would otherwise have.

At 1.3 miles, water flows over the sandstone, creating modest Chapel Falls. Navigate around the edge of the escarpment. Your trail narrows as it squeezes among some moderate-sized white pines before you end up back on a wide, straight, and flat trail. Enjoy root-free footing as you approach the beach. The footpath becomes narrower in some places. This provides for a more intimate experience as you wind your way through the forest, intermittently grasping trees and getting to know them a little better.

Bikes are prohibited on this wilderness trail, allowing for a quality experience. Because you are in prime bear and wolf country, no dogs are allowed, either. A dog in the backcountry, coming nose to nose with a bear, or worse, a wolf, could spell doom for the dog and a miserable and dangerous experience for the owner.

As you approach the beach, the elevation declines slightly, and you'll notice American beech trees, yellow birches, and noticeably fewer sugar maples. You'll also

see a new tree species, striped maple, a definite sign of a more boreal forest. Keep your eyes on the canopy overhead, and watch it begin to open up as you continue your trek to the northeast.

At 2.9 miles, climb down a timber staircase shortly after the canopy yields blue skies, and 0.2 mile later, you are standing in front of Chapel Rock, a large sandstone formation with a white pine precariously perched on top. The lapping (or roaring) sounds of Lake Superior invite you to turn west and step carefully along the sandy escarpment 20 feet above the water.

The trail here is sandy, with some roots and a few rocks. This is inconsequential, as you'll be afforded some of the best views of the Pictured Rocks sandstone formations. Although you cannot see it from here, Grand Portal Point is just around the corner from the sandstone cliffs you do see. Venture down to the beach using one of the dedicated access trails. As you walk west, the sand beach abruptly ends at the sandstone face rising over 100 feet in front of you.

Look around at the white pine, red pine, white spruce, mountain ash, blueberry bushes, and mosses. The trail goes by the Chapel Lake backcountry campsites. Just 0.3 mile after reaching the beach and passing the campsites, you will turn inland. The habitat is noticeably dry, with lots of bracken fern and soggy sand footing. There is even a boardwalk several hundred feet long to keep you out of the sand until you get about 0.2 mile away from the beach.

Continue your flat walk, passing Little Chapel Lake on your right. Beyond the lake, the habitat starts to take on its familiar northern hardwood forest appearance, with more paper birch and yellow birch. Barely 0.5 mile from the beach, you are fully engulfed again by the sugar maple-dominated hardwood forest.

The ground underfoot becomes a hard-packed two-track. There's an ever-so-subtle increase in elevation for the next 0.5 mile. At 1.5 miles from the beach, you'll find yourself on the edge of an escarpment. This is where you get your one and only view of Chapel Lake.

Continue your current pace on the mostly flat trail, with a few slight rises. You will come to a 20-foot decline where the trail corridor narrows and the forest becomes thick with balsam fir. You are about 0.3 mile from the parking area and 0.1 mile from the Mosquito Loop–Chapel Loop intersection (see Hikes 42 and 47).

The remaining trail is rockier and quite wide. After crossing a small stream on a footbridge, you will turn toward the parking lot, climb slightly (notice the cedar trees in the area), and end at your vehicle.

41

Grand Island Loop

*Place: Grand Island National
Recreation Area*

Total distance: 7.4 miles

Hiking time: 3–5 hours

Gradient: Easy

*High points: Easy-to-follow trails, rock
outcroppings, remote*

*Maps: USGS 7.5' Munising; Grand Island
National Recreation Area map*

*Amenities: Pit toilets and water at
trailhead*

Footwear: Tennis shoes

Pets: Yes

SUMMARY

Grand Island was rescued from the impending doom of potentially being developed in the late 1980s. The Trust for Public Land, a private, nonprofit organization, purchased the land and then sold it to the federal government to be made into a recreation area. It is now part of the Hiawatha National Forest.

For years, the island was the property of William Mather, owner of the Cleveland-Cliffs Company. The trails on the island are all remnants of old roads that Mather and his guests once used.

This is a quick and easy trek, and a good choice if you are looking to get away from crowds, and be assured you will not get lost. The island is very peaceful, and it's quite easy to find your way around. Island trails are wide and well maintained, and relatively few visitors hike them. Vehicles are allowed on the island, but it's not likely you will encounter any on this hike. Bikes, however, are allowed on most of the trails, and you will likely encounter them, as this is a popular destination for cyclists.

This loop will take you mostly through maturing forests and along cliffs bordering Lake Superior. Take the time to familiarize yourself with the names of various roads, trails, campgrounds, and points of interest on the island, as each intersection on the island is signed and gives distances to many of these places. Most of these features do not appear on the basic map you will receive on the ferry.

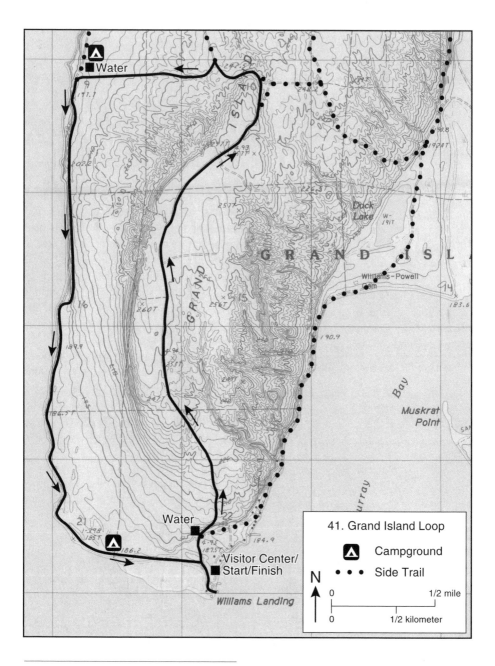

41. Grand Island Loop

🏕 Campground

• • • Side Trail

N

0   1/2 mile

0   1/2 kilometer

ACCESS

From Munising, take M 28 west 3 miles to the Grand Island Recreation Area marina. There is a ferry operated by concession, which operates from the Friday of Memorial Day weekend through the beginning of October. (For more information and departure times, call the Grand Island Ferry

Service at 906-387-3503.) The ferry ride takes only 10 minutes from mainland to the island.

THE TRAIL

After arriving at a modest dock, take the wooden boardwalk to an even more modest ranger station, just an old wooden building with some interpretive panels telling the history of the island. Since Grand Island can be buggy, the screened-in room may offer an insect-free oasis before you embark on your trek.

Veer left toward the pit toilets, and look for the sign that reads "all trails." This is the beginning of Center Trail, which is a gravel road open to bikes and motor vehicles. At 0.1 mile is a gate off to your left—this is where you will also end today. There is a hand water pump available. At 0.2 mile, the road splits. Take the gravel road to the left and continue uphill at an easy to moderate grade for nearly 2 miles.

The habitat is mostly young northern hardwood forest, chiefly American beech and some sugar maple. If you look closely into the forest, you will notice many old stumps. When William Mather passed away in 1952, there was a dispute over ownership of the island between his estate and his company, Cleveland-Cliffs. Cleveland-Cliffs quickly harvested most of the trees the year after his death, denuding the island of most of its mature forest. Today, this impact is very noticeable, not only from the stumps, but in that there are so many small trees scrambling to reach the canopy for a smidgen of sunlight. As you hike, you may wonder which trees will make it and which will not over the next two hundred years before this forest reaches a mature climax.

The road is generally straight and wide, with a gentle grade. Since it so little used and lightly maintained, many of the native wildflowers have encroached on its edges.

In late summer, the wildlife seems more active than on the mainland. Keep your eyes open for red-eyed vireos, bald eagles, double-crested cormorants, waterfowl, gulls, and hawks. Pileated woodpeckers searching for insects have created many large, rectangular holes in dead and dying beech trees.

This is one of those times when you will think you have reached the top, and the trail takes a slight bend and continues to climb. Thankfully, the grade is gentle and the footing is easy on the feet.

At the top is an abundant growth of an uncommon Upper Peninsula plant, ninebark. Although shade intolerant, it seems to be flourishing along the roads on the island. Ninebark is one of our smallest woody plants, a shrub if you will, and its bark can peel off, exposing a brown, inner bark. It has showy white flowers and large, simple, alternating leaves. Its red fruit is ripe in late summer.

Reach the apex in an open field and the terrain becomes flat, reentering the woods in 0.1 mile. The young forest stretches its branches over the road, as if they are shaking hands with each other. Elderberry, maidenhair fern, evergreen woodfern, jewelweed, goldenrods, wintergreen, bunchberry, sarsaparilla, and large-leaved aster make up the undergrowth.

Look for glacial erratics (scattered boulders left behind as the glaciers retreated), and in 0.3 mile, you will start going downhill 0.1 mile to a Y-intersection. Take the left fork 0.1 mile to the intersection with Old East-West Road. Turn left, and in 0.1 mile, the road bends around to the right. You will take a two-track to your left, which is at the 2.8-mile mark into your journey. This little-used road is still open to vehicles, although it looks unmaintained.

Head west, rise and fall for 0.3 mile, then level out to a slight downhill grade through mixed forest until you come to the intersection with West Rim Trail in 0.5 mile. Turn left, head south, and you will be paralleling the shore, although you will only get glimpses of it for the next mile or so. This is because the steep drop obscures your outlook through the thick forest, further blocking your view of Lake Superior.

This trail is open to pedestrians and bicycles but not motor vehicles. In the winter, snowmobiles also use this pathway. From the trail intersection with Old East-West Road back to the ferry dock is 3 miles.

Continue to hug the shore. There is a very gradual downhill grade, and the trail will come close enough to the edge to get views of the lake. There are several places where fences have been established, mostly to alert snowmobilers to these drop-offs.

Your only beach access is at Merchandise Point, 2 miles from the previous trail intersection and 1 mile from the end. A short boardwalk leads to the beach. The trail then bends due east toward Williams Landing. Note that the forest here has a boreal feel, with the appearance of mountain ash and abundant balsam fir. You will reach Center Road, turn right, and it is 0.1 mile to the ranger station and boat dock.

42

Grand Portal Point

Place: Pictured Rocks National Lakeshore

Total distance: 9.1 miles

Hiking time: 5–8 hours

Gradient: Moderate

High points: Wilderness setting, geological formations

Maps: USGS 7.5' Grand Portal Point; NCT MI-10; Pictured Rocks Chapel Basin Day Hikes map

Amenities: Bathrooms at trailhead. Bathrooms and camping at Mosquito Beach and Chapel Beach

Footwear: Backpacking boots

Pets: Prohibited and illegal

SUMMARY

Using part of the Chapel Lake and Mosquito Loop, access the stretch of the Lakeshore Trail that curves around Grand Portal Point, a 100-foot-high sandstone formation that juts over Lake Superior.

The footing is mostly loose sand and comes precariously close to the fragile edge of the formations, so take heed—this can be a dangerous adventure at times. Resist the temptation to walk to the edge for that photo op!

The forest, the sandstone formations, and the turquoise waters of Lake Superior give visual splendor to this hike.

ACCESS

From Munising, take H-58 east and turn north onto Chapel Road, following the signs for Grand Portal Point until the road ends.

THE TRAIL

Use the 1.9-mile trail consisting of the north loop of the Mosquito Beach and Falls Trail to gain access to Mosquito Beach. Take the Lakeshore Trail 0.1 mile to the right and head northeast and begin your climb to the sandstone formations.

You will mostly be hugging the edge, with a smattering of trees including mountain ash and balsam fir between you and a 100-foot plunge into the lake. Your footing is sandy and the trail occasionally jogs inland to avoid especially fragile areas.

You are walking along the Au Train Formation, which is relatively resistant to erosion. This 450-million-year-old formation

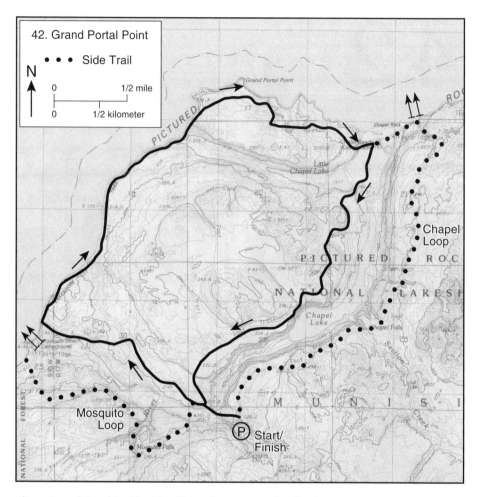

42. Grand Portal Point

• • • Side Trail

N

0 .... 1/2 mile

0 .... 1/2 kilometer

Grand Portal Point

PICTURED

Chapel Rock

Little Chapel Lake

Chapel Loop

PICTURED   ROC

NATIONAL   LAKESH

Chapel Lake

Chapel Falls

Mosquito Beach Campground

NATIONAL FOREST

Mosquito Loop

Mosquito Falls

P Start/ Finish

M U N I S

sits on top of the older Munising Formation. The Munising formation is quite prone to erosion.

Grand Portal Point and Miners Castle are both formed from Miners Castle sandstone (see Hikes 43 and 45). When you get to the trail turning inland on the Chapel Loop, take in Chapel Rock, which is made of Chapel Rock sandstone, the next layer below the Munising formation, and considerably harder and more durable.

This whole area was once covered by an ancient sea, dubbed the Late Cambrian Munising Sea. Sediments from the sur-

rounding landscape settled at the bottom, creating the geology lying underfoot.

This particular Pictured Rocks trail has a noticeable boreal feel to it. The sandy soils are poor in nutrients, and the lake keeps the area cool and wet, which encourages boreal vegetation to take hold in this particular area.

At the 1.8-mile mark, descend into what appears to be an old river basin. You will negotiate this quickly, and in 0.2 mile, you will be back up along the edge.

Note the preponderance of white spruce and balsam fir, two key boreal trees. Both

Sandstone formations make the pictured rocks

these evergreens are more prevalent than you might expect in a typical UP forest. There are also abundant lichens and mosses clinging onto the bark, branches, and needles of the evergreens.

The boreal feel comes from the mountain ash and mountain maple trees, and blueberries. Mountain ash is a small tree with a typical spreading crown. It has showy white flowers and bright red, clumped berries in the late summer and fall. Its compound leaf looks like a small version of a sumac leaf, and its berries attract wildlife, even moose. Moose will also eat mountain ash in the winter, browsing on the fragrant bark.

Mountain maple leaves resemble those of the striped maple, and look like an oversized goose foot. Mountain maple is shade-tolerant, slow-growing, and short-lived shrub. Although it does produce the characteristic "helicopter" seeds common to other maples, its primary method of reproduction is vegeta-

tively, by spreading and layering its roots in new areas.

There are more than 10 species of blueberry in Michigan. Two prevalent varieties are velvetleaf and low sweet blueberry. As you swat away the blackflies, thank them—as they are the primary pollinators of the blueberries that provide you a late summer treat.

Turn east and cut through the forest dominated by red maple. The trail comes out very close to the edge, giving you great views of the Caribbean-colored water, which is the backdrop for Grand Portal Point.

Again, be careful not to fall off the edge! The lake has sculpted the sandstone creating several concave indentations into the cliff face.

At the 3.3-mile mark, the trail starts descending through the forest toward Chapel Beach, where it ends. Turn right (south) on the northern Chapel Beach circuit and head 3.1 miles back to the trailhead.

43

Lakeshore Trail

Place: Pictured Rocks National Lakeshore

Total distance: 42.4 miles

Hiking time: 4–6 days

Gradient: Moderate with some difficult climbs

High points: Wilderness setting with rock formations, remote beaches, and unspoiled habitats

Maps: USGS 7.5' Pictured Rocks, Indiantown, Wood Island NE, Grand Portal Point, Au Sable Point, Trappers Lake, Grand Sable Lake; North Country Trail map MI-10

Amenities: Numerous backcountry campsites with some pit and composting toilets. Leave No Trace methods required.

Footwear: Backpacking boots

Pets: Prohibited and illegal

SUMMARY

If you are going to go backpacking once in your life, this route should be among your top five choices due to its ease and accessibility. Each year, more than 10,000 backpackers register to drag themselves a few miles or sprint the entire length of the Lakeshore Trail, making this route one of the most popular stretches on the entire 4,500-mile North Country Trail.

Starting at Munising Falls, you'll progress northeast, mostly along the high escarpments at the edge of Lake Superior. The trail comes down to the lake only a handful of times until you reach the Beaver Lake area. Then, the trail hugs the sandy Twelvemile Beach until Log Slide, where it turns inland, travels between Grand Sable Dunes and Grand Sable Lake, and ends at the Grand Sable visitor center.

There is frequent disagreement among different maps, guides, and trail signs regarding distances between waypoints on the Lakeshore Trail. These differences should not negatively affect your experience.

In addition to the usual Leave No Trace practices, there are other backcountry regulations for Pictured Rocks. The most important are:

1. Permits are required for backcountry camping. These can be obtained at either visitor center.
2. No mechanized vehicles or pets are allowed in the backcountry.
3. You must camp at designated campsites only.
4. Stay away from the edges of cliffs, as they are made of fragile sandstone.

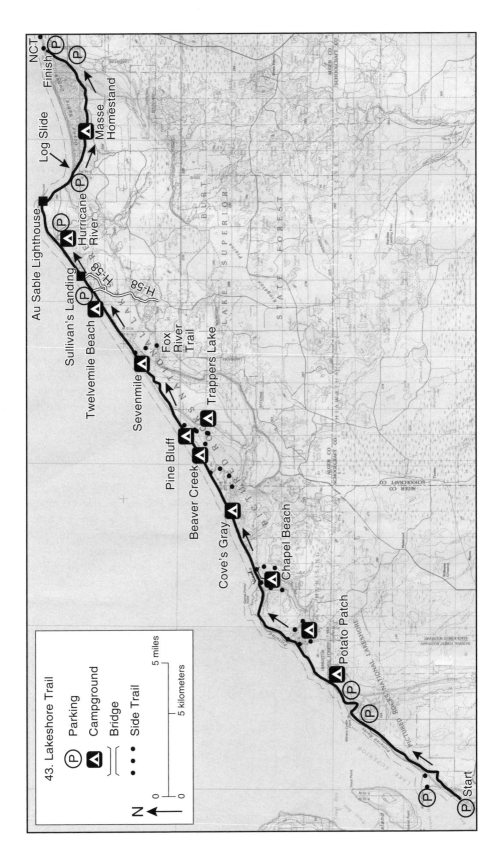

43. Lakeshore Trail

N ←

P Parking
▲ Campground
⊓ Bridge
• • • Side Trail

0   5 miles
0   5 kilometers

Start
P
P
Potato Patch
Chapel Beach
Cove's Gray
Beaver Creek
Pine Bluff
Sevenmile
Trappers Lake
Fox River Trail
Twelvemile Beach
Sullivan's Landing
H-58
Hurricane River
Au Sable Lighthouse
Log Slide
Masse Homestand
Finish
NCT
P
P
P
P
P

LAKE SUPERIOR

PICTURED ROCKS NATIONAL LAKESHORE

HIAWATHA NATIONAL FOREST

BURT STATE FOREST

SCHOOLCRAFT CO
ALGER CO

MUNISING

ACCESS

From Munising, take H 58 east 2 miles, and turn left onto Sand Point Road. Follow Sand Point Road and park at Munising Falls. The trailhead is adjacent to the interpretive building. Altran (Alger County Public Transportation) offers a backpacker shuttle. Inquire at the ranger station for dates and times.

THE TRAIL

Day 1

Your quest starts at Munising Falls, a popular way station for tourists looking for a short tramp along the shore. Hit the ground running, and within 500 feet, you will have the forest all to yourself. In the next mile, you will have reached the edge of the escarpment and gained several hundred feet in elevation. For the next 42 miles, you will be looking down on Lake Superior, and walking in and out of a northern hardwood forest that seems to be fighting its northern boreal counterpart.

At 2 miles, you'll notice Sand Point jutting out into South Bay, pointing toward Grand Island. High up on the escarpment, a side trail to Sand Point joins the Lakeshore Trail at 2.9 miles into your journey. It is a steep descent to Sand Point, if you are inclined to take a side trip so early in your adventure.

Wind in and out of the woods, hugging the escarpment, and you will see places where the trail has slipped into Lake Superior. You reach Cliff Campsites after 5.1 miles, and Cliffs Group sites at the 6.4-mile marker. Note that water isn't available at Cliff Campsites. Perched high above the lake, this is a great vantage point from which to witness a Lake Superior sunset.

Miners Castle, the most popular destination at Pictured Rocks National Lakeshore, is next. The trail is lined with poison ivy

about 0.25 mile before this waypoint, so tread carefully. Emerge from the woods at the 7-mile mark, and you'll be greeted by a sea of humanity on any summer day with decent weather. Miners Castle is composed of two kinds of sandstone, Miners and Chapel, and the formation once had two turrets on top. (The northeast turret collapsed on April 13, 2006.) A small interpretive site, bathrooms, and even "backpacker parking" greet you here. Take in the view, then follow the paved trail downhill for an up-close view of the castle.

Leave the pavement behind and descend a steep embankment, crossing the Miners River. Follow the beach, but only 20 or so feet above Lake Superior. At 8.8 miles, is a parking lot, at which you start your climb back up the escarpment. At 8.9 miles, you'll reach Potato Patch. This backcountry campsite has no water, so make sure to load up on water at Miners River or from Lake Superior soon after passing the river.

Day 2

Fortunately, your next encampment will offer easy access to water. After a good night's sleep at Potato Patch, stay up on the cliff for several miles. At 11.5 miles, start descending to Mosquito Campsites, River, and Beach. At 12 miles you'll reach the mouth of the Mosquito River, where you can swim in a shallow and potentially warm bay, although Lake Superior rarely gets above 45 degrees even in the summer. After your swim, cross the river on the footbridge, follow the beach, and begin a moderate ascent back up to the top of the escarpment. Prepare yourself for the most spectacular views so far, as you will be tramping around Grand Portal Point. The aquamarine water juxtaposed with the reddish sandstone allows you to comprehend why this area is called Pictured Rocks.

Lakeshore Trail

You reach Chapel Beach at the 16.4-mile mark, but not before a 0.4-mile steep decline down and around the edge of the escarpment. Cross the Chapel River, then, at 16.7 miles, admire the lone white pine tree perched atop Chapel Rock.

Climb back up the escarpment. The trail continues mostly in the woods, but comes to the edge often enough to give you great views. At 18.4 miles, cross Spray Creek, where a social side trail attempts to bring you to Spray Falls. This is not recommended! The only way you can safely get a quality view of the falls is by taking the concessionaire boat ride (Pictured Rocks Cruises, www.picturedrocks.com). The social trail would have you balancing on fragile sandstone, risking a fatal plunge.

Coves Group (no water) and Coves Campsites are at 19.2 and 20.7 miles, respectively. When you reach Coves Campsite, you will have descended from the high cliffs and notice the beginnings of a sandy

beach. This is one end of Twelvemile Beach, and plenty of access to water.

The coves may be lightly used—however, you will notice many backpackers congregating around the Beaver Lake and Beaver Creek areas. At 22 miles, Beaver Creek is a popular destination, because it is accessible from a nearby parking lot. Be prepared to share your campsite.

Day 3

Today, take a break from two days of serious hiking with a short trek. Pass Pine Bluff campsites at 23.5 miles and Trappers Lake Trail at 24.4 miles and you will turn inland just before you reach Sevenmile Creek Campground at the 28-mile mark. This is a remarkable campground, heavily wooded with some decent sandstone outcroppings.

Set up camp in the shadow of the outcroppings near the shore of raging Sevenmile Creek. If you brought your fishing pole, try your hand at catching a native brook trout. If geology is your bag, you have plenty of sandstone to keep you busy. On the other hand, pull out a good book and take it easy for the rest of the day.

Day 4

Continue the adventure and pass the intersection to the Fox River Pathway at the 28.4-mile mark. Look uphill and reconsider what would be three-day toil to Seney, the next town to the south.

You will notice that the landscape rises appreciably to your right as you continue your low walk along the beach. At 30.9-mile mark, walk into Twelvemile Beach Campground. Amenities here include potable water, pit toilets, and an interpretive kiosk.

Leave the campground loop, and the trail will lead you through a gate, off road, and into the woods, but only for about 0.5 mile. In the meantime, look for Benchmark (a backcountry campsite) at the 31.2-mile mark before finding yourself on H-58, which is soon to be paved. Hopefully, the road engineers will separate the Lakeshore Trail appropriately, putting it into the woods rather than on the current road.

At 32.5 miles, leave H-58 and reenter the woods, continuing to parallel Lake Superior. Hurricane River Campground (rustic) is at the 33.7-mile mark. Again, walk the campground loop drive until you reach a gate, which is the access to the Au Sable Light Station (see Hike 39). The corridor to the light station is flat, wide, and well used, and you will reach the lighthouse at 33.7 miles. This will be your last access to water for the next 8 miles, until you reach Grand Sable Lake.

Turn southeast, and you will pass the easternmost part of Au Sable Point, where the footing will become noticeably sandy and a higher concentration of poison ivy is evident. Log Slide, a place where loggers ingeniously slid lumber down the steep slopes of the Grand Sable Dunes, is your next landmark at the 37.1-mile mark.

Reenter the woods and negotiate the inland side of the Grand Sable Dunes while occasionally slogging through sand. Masse Homestead, your last backcountry camp, is at the 38.3-mile mark. There is no water access at this campsite.

Day 5

By now, you should be well versed in making sure you have enough water when you camp at the sites that have no access to Lake Superior or its tributaries. It's ironic that you have the world's largest lake just on the other side of this wooded dune, but you are constantly worrying about having enough water!

Trek though the woods as the trail skirts H-58 and crosses over the highway north of Grand Sable Lake. Your hike ends at the Grand Sable Visitor Center, at the 42.4-mile mark. Congratulations—make sure to purchase your commemorative patch at the gift shop in the visitor center.

44

Log Slide Overlook

Place: Pictured Rocks National Lakeshore

Total distance: 0.4 mile

Hiking time: ½ hour

Gradient: Easy

High points: View of Grand Sable Dunes

Maps: USGS 7.5' Grand Sable Lake; NCT MI-10

Amenities: Pit toilets

Footwear: Flip-flops

Pets: Allowed in parking area only, not on the trail

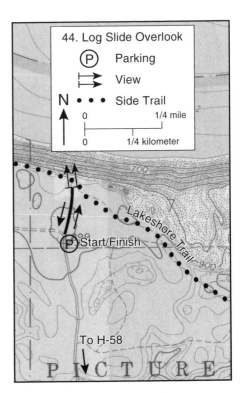

SUMMARY

This is a short trail to a viewing platform overlooking Lake Superior, Grand Sable Banks, and Grand Sable Dunes. To the west is the Au Sable Light Station. An optional trip to the bottom of the dunes is possible, but is only for those in excellent physical condition.

ACCESS

From Grand Marais, take H-58 west 10 miles. Turn north on road marked for Log Slide and follow it until it ends at a parking lot.

Grand Sable Banks

THE TRAIL

From an improved parking area, the wide, packed gravel path starts in the hardwood forest. You'll pass an outbuilding with some historic logging artifacts, and then the forest canopy disappears and the footing becomes sandy. The North Country Trail crosses the trail at this point; you have the choice of walking up the backside of what appears to be a dune on your right. On your left is a boardwalk that ends at an overlook.

Be very careful in this area, especially with pets. Poison ivy, a member of the cashew family, proliferates in just about every possible place. Park regulations require you to keep pets on a leash, but you will need someone to wait with Fido at the parking area. Although your dog will not be affected by poison ivy, the urushiol (the plant's oil that causes the infamous rash) he picks up can be easily transmitted to you and your family.

Take the trail to the overlook, for wide and expansive vistas of Au Sable Point, Grand Sable Dunes, Grand Sable Banks, and, of course, the world's largest freshwater lake!

This is the approximate location of the famous Log Slide. Lumbermen would send large logs down a wooden chute to waiting schooners. These boats would then tow the logs to Grand Marais to be processed in mills. Legend has it that the logs were so heavy and moved so fast downhill that the sluice would catch fire.

After turning back, you are tempted to climb the 20 feet up the small sandy hill on your left. The top affords you yet another view, and a stern warning about descending to Lake Superior.

The descent looks easy. However, the dune is pitched at such an angle that it is easy to dislodge rocks and sand, causing an avalanche of sorts. The climb back up, to be kind, is extremely strenuous and should be attempted only by those in excellent physical shape. There are many stories of unprepared and out-of-shape beachcombers who suffered a lapse in judgment and had to be rescued. If you do decide to descend the 300 feet to the shore, it will feel like a thousand climbing back up. Think twice before departing.

45

Miners Beach to Miners Castle

Place: Pictured Rocks National Lakeshore

Total distance: 2.4 miles round trip

Hiking time: 2 hours

Gradient: Mostly difficult, some easy stretches

High points: Sandstone formations, remote beach

Maps: USGS 7.5' Indiantown; North Country Trail MI-10

Amenities: Picnic areas, bathrooms at both trailheads

Footwear: Hiking boots

Pets: Allowed on beach and in parking areas. Not allowed on trail.

SUMMARY

The Miners Castle to Miners Beach route is a popular hike. Most hikers start from Miners Castle, which is higher in elevation. Of course this is perfectly acceptable, but you may be better off starting at Miners Beach and laboring uphill, guaranteeing that your return journey will lead downhill.

The beach is popular with picnickers, and Miners Castle is probably the most popular destination in the Painted Rocks National Lakeshore. There is a significant climb in elevation in a very short stretch of trail, so plan accordingly.

ACCESS

From Munising, take H-58 east to H-13, turn north, take it until it comes to an intersection, turn right, and take it to the bottom of the hill. Turn left at the intersection and park at the end of the road.

THE TRAIL

Miners Beach recently underwent major improvements to its parking lots and bathroom facilities. Park personnel have also installed many fences, walkways, and boardwalks to encourage visitors to stay on improved paths and discourage going off trail. The habitat in this area is mostly jackpine forest with fragile lichens as groundcover. In dry weather, lichens are easily damaged, so always stay on the maintained trails and avoid using or creating social trails.

From the west end of the parking area, take the wooden boardwalk straight to the beach. If you brought your charcoal and grilling supplies, you can enjoy a delicious

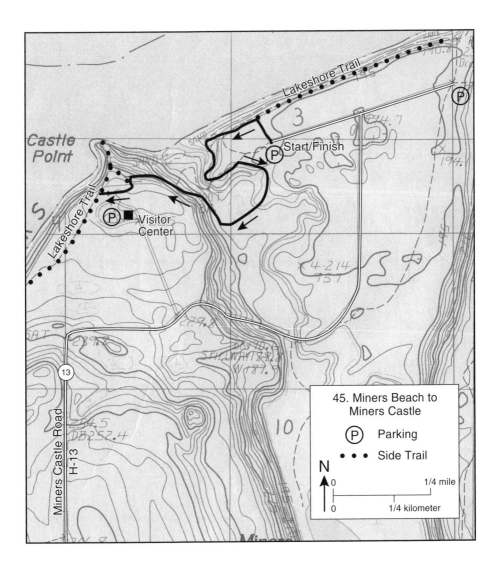

45. Miners Beach to
Miners Castle

Ⓟ Parking

• • • Side Trail

N

0   1/4 mile
0   1/4 kilometer

barbecue. There are numerous picnic tables and grills in the vicinity.

The boardwalk ends in 0.1 mile at a
sandy bluff where there is a set of wooden
stairs leading to the beach. Resist the temptation to swim in the 45-degree water and
turn left, keeping Lake Superior's cool waters on your right. The trail is scantily
marked along this stretch, but rest assured
that you are on the Lakeshore Trail headed
west toward Miners Castle.

Within a few hundred feet, a small sign
indicates that you have 1 mile to Miners
Castle. The habitat along the beach is
sandy, sporting mostly red pines and jackpines, which thrive in these dry soils.
Blueberry plants are plentiful, but the
berries themselves may not be due to casual connoisseurs of this delicious berry
taking some for a tasty treat.

Come to a bluff, and you will find many
social trails nearby. Keep the bluff on your

Miners Castle

right as the trail bends away from the lake and another sign (Lakeshore Trail–Miners River) points you in the correct direction.

The tread is wide, sandy, and often covered in pine needles, making for a comfortable walk. Descend into a small gully and you'll find another sign directing you to Miners Castle. Cross Miners River and then walk parallel to the river on a wide trail that is rooty in spots. Just 0.2 mile from the Miners River, the trail starts its ascent up to Miners Castle. The escarpment is on your left and is forested mostly by paper birch and sugar maples. Once you cross over a small footbridge, your climb really begins. For the next 0.7 mile, you will be switchbacking, scrambling, and trying not to lose your footing in the soil. Remnants of the sandstone formation making up the Pictured Rocks, the sand loosely fills in where roots are exposed.

With 0.1 mile remaining in your climb, you'll reach an asphalt trail coming from the summit, intersecting with your rooty and sandy trail. To the right is a close-up view of Miners Castle. Head to the left, and switchback up to the grassy open area and an overlook that gives you great pause as you think of how long nature took to create this wonder.

Those who have visited Miners Castle in the past will notice that one of the turrets has disappeared! Although Miners Castle was not as famous as the Old Man of the Mountain in New Hampshire (which collapsed on May 3, 2003), when the northeast turret of Miners Castle fell into Lake Superior on April 13, 2006, it made the news all over Michigan. Erosion is not only the force that created these geologic features, but it also wears them away. Retrace your steps to return to your car.

46

Miners Falls

Place: Pictured Rocks National Lakeshore

Total distance: 1.2 miles round trip

Hiking time: 45 minutes

Gradient: Easy

High points: Waterfall, American yew, sandstone formations

Maps: USGS 7.5' Indiantown

Amenities: Pit toilets, picnic area, grills, interpretive brochure

Footwear: Tennis shoes

Pets: Prohibited and illegal

SUMMARY

Though this is technically a backcountry trail, many people interested in viewing Miners Falls make this very popular with day users to Pictured Rocks. A gentle downhill slope takes you to an observation platform and a staircase offering good views not only of the waterfall, but also of the geological formation that makes is so impressive.

English geologists–employees of Alexander Henry who were exploring the area around 1772–named the Miners River because the tannins staining the water led them to believe there might be minerals in the region. Though no minerals were ever found or excavated, the name stuck.

ACCESS

From Munising, take H-58 east 5 miles, turning north onto Miners Road. The road to Miners Falls is on the right in 4 miles.

THE TRAIL

Your footing on this hike consists of crushed gravel and makes for an easy, gradual downhill walk. A brochure rack at the trailhead correlates with 12 numbered posts detailing the natural and cultural history of the area.

As the trail continues downhill, notice that the land falls away from you on both sides. Glaciers sculpted the landscape 10,000 years ago, and Lake Superior filled the area when water levels were much higher. Today, the land is covered in typical, northern hardwood forest, mostly sugar maples and some beeches.

In May, spring ephemerals typical of such a forest are in full bloom. Hepaticas,

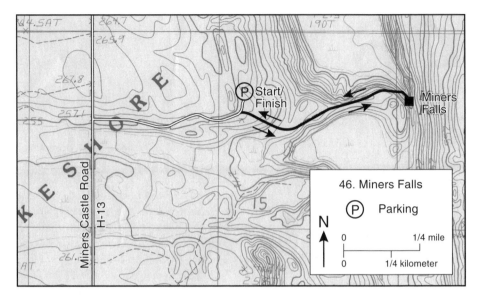

46. Miners Falls

P Parking

N

0 ——————— 1/4 mile

0 ——————— 1/4 kilometer

spring beauties, trout lilies, and the uncommon bloodroot bloom until the forest is fully leafed, which occurs in June.

At station #3, take note of the evergreen shrub covering the ground. Does it look similar to something growing under the windows of your home? American yew is a close relative of the Japanese yew, which many of us have adorning our foundations. This very slow-growing, long-lived, shade-tolerant shrub is very hardy—except to the browsing of white-tailed deer, which find American yew a favorite food.

A keen eye will notice northern cedar, another popular food for white-tailed deer, growing in this area as well.

The abundance of these two preferred deer foods tells a story about which animals are here and which are not. If deer were present in any numbers, American yew and northern cedar would be nonexistent, or very sparse. The fact that they are so abundant tells us that deer are relatively scarce.

Why are there so few deer? One reason is that this region does receive a lot of snow, and both American yew and northern cedar could be buried and inaccessible in winter. The other reason is that wolves and bears, the two main predators of deer, are present in the park and work in conjunction with the harsh climate to keep deer populations in check.

Come to a split-rail fence on your left, indicating the end of the trail and two opportunities to view Miners Falls. A staircase leading down the side of the sandstone escarpment offers the better viewing opportunity, but makes your hike more strenuous: you'll have just over 50 steps to climb back to the top. Even if you are not a fan of waterfalls, the escarpment is covered with fascinating plants clinging to a meager existence. Polystichum fern, sometimes known as Christmas fern, dominates. There are lichens and mosses apparently glued to the rock face, fighting gravity for all they are worth. An observation platform is available, but the view of Miners Falls free-falling water is mostly obscured by trees. The falls is the 11th station. Retrace your steps to return to your car.

Miners Falls

47

Mosquito Falls and Beach Loop

Place: Pictured Rocks National Lakeshore

Total distance: 4.5 miles

Hiking time: 2–4 hours

Gradient: Easy

High points: Waterfall, wilderness backcountry including beach and sandstone formations

Maps: USGS 7.5' Grand Portal Point, Pictured Rocks National Lakeshore map; Pictured Rocks Chapel Basin Day Hikes map; NCT MI-10

Amenities: Bathrooms at trailhead and beach. Mosquito Beach has a backcountry campground available by permit only.

Footwear: Hiking boots

Pets: Prohibited and illegal

SUMMARY

This surprisingly flat trek takes you past the impressive, cascading Mosquito Falls, then down to Mosquito Beach and the mouth of the Mosquito River. You will pass through mature hardwood forests. The habitat is generally moist—keep in mind that this area has "mosquito" as its moniker for a reason!

The beach is remote and sandy, and the warmer waters of the Mosquito River discharge into a small, shallow bay, which in late summer is warm enough to swim in. To the northeast of the mouth, small sandstone formations are worthy of exploring.

Maps, signs, and even the Pictured Rocks National Lakeshore's own "official" trail distances disagree with each other about the distances between waypoints. These differences are minor and should not cause any concern.

ACCESS

From Munising, take H-58 east and turn left (north) onto Chapel Road, following the signs until it ends.

THE TRAIL

If you have already hiked Chapel Falls Loop or Grand Portal Point, you will recognize the beginning of your next adventure, as it is the last 0.3 mile of a hike already taken (see Hikes 40 and 42). The path is very wide, and in places your footing is rocky. You will cross a small gully with an intermittent stream and head back up into mature woods. At 0.3 mile is a sign directing you left for Mosquito Falls and Beach, or right for Chapel Beach.

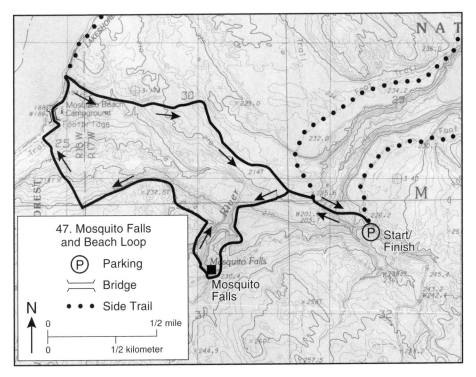

**47. Mosquito Falls
and Beach Loop**

(P) Parking

⌐⌐ Bridge

• • • Side Trail

N

0		1/2 mile
0	1/2 kilometer	

Like most of the trails in Pictured Rocks, these are well worn and without any directional markings. At 0.1 mile from the intersection with the Chapel Falls Loop is a sign indicating that Mosquito Falls is 0.8 mile from here. The forest consists of balsam fir, red maple, sugar maple, large hemlock, yellow birch, and a little smattering of beech trees.

The forest battles between the dominant mesic northern hardwoods and the boreal characteristics encouraged by the cold and moisture brought by the close proximity of Lake Superior. Balsam fir, goldthread, striped maple, and mountain ash–all boreal species–eke out their existence along the edge of the immense lake. Watch your step to avoid Clintonia and clubmoss under a canopy of hemlock and sugar maple.

Descend carefully, watching for rooty underfooting, and at 0.5 mile from the last intersection, the trail swings more to the north. The Mosquito River basin is evident on your left–this does not seem correct, but the trail doesn't lie and sometimes will not reveal its secrets until later. For the next 0.3 mile, work your way upstream, eventually turning so you parallel the Mosquito River on your right, through rather steep and moderately difficult climbs. Soon you will hear the low roar of the falls. However, the next descent is down and then up through a small gully, containing a feeder creek to the Mosquito. The climb back up to the top of the escarpment is quite steep.

After a hairpin turn, notice a set of three waterfalls to your right. You can choose from one of many social trails down to the water's edge. The upper and lower cascades are about 15 feet in height. The middle cascade is about 5 feet in height.

About 100 yards past the upper falls, cross a footbridge and parallel the river

Mouth of the Mosquito River

downstream. Again, you will be climbing elevation to get back to the top of the escarpment, and then the trail levels out.

For the next 1.6 miles, parallel the river, which is now off in the distance. The trail is mostly wide and has occasional slight declines as you approach the beach. Be aware of several intersecting two-tracks, which are marked, and follow the designated trail markers. Keep your eye to the sky, as when the canopy starts letting in more light, you are near the beach.

At the intersection with the Lakeshore Trail are signs directing you to a group campsite and the Lakeshore Trail itself. You will turn right and head for the mouth of the Mosquito River. Boreal forest dominates right along the edge of the lake, and the hike may make you feel as if you are in northern Canada, not the Upper Peninsula.

Descend in elevation, and skirt the campground to reach the river. Enjoy the sandy beach and sandstone formations,

and take a swim if you have the time. Cross the Mosquito on a small footbridge and immediately come to the only sign that jives with the trail map. The Lakeshore Trail is straight ahead, and the Mosquito Loop turns inland to your right. The sign and map indicate a 1.9-mile jaunt to the parking area.

The forest quickly regains its northern hardwood character 0.1 mile from the intersection. So much for the boreal forest. Your return route to the parking area is an ever so slight incline through mature forest. About 0.5 mile in, cross a small gully, then enter a thick and swampy area on an old logging road. A few puncheons will help you traverse some low, wet spots. About 0.2 mile from the start of the Mosquito Loop, descend about 20 feet through some young forest and back to level footing and to the beginning of the loop. It is 0.1 mile back to the intersection with Chapel Loop and 0.3 mile to the parking area.

48

Munising Falls

Place: Pictured Rocks National Lakeshore

Total distance: 0.4 mile round trip

Hiking time: ½ hour

Gradient: Easy to moderate

High points: Waterfall, intimate views of sandstone formations

Maps: USGS 7.5' Indiantown

Amenities: Small interpretive center, modern bathrooms

Footwear: Flip-flops

Pets: Yes

48. Munising Falls

Ⓟ   Parking

• • • Side Trail

N

0   1/4 mile

0   1/4 kilometer

SUMMARY

This short leg stretcher takes you to the base of Munising Falls. There are two staircases, one on each side of the falls, which you can take up for a bird's eye view and have a close encounter with the sandstone formations.

The beauty of the Pictured Rocks and attractions like Munising Falls make for a great geology lesson. Ancient seas covered the Great Lakes from about 600 to 500 million years ago. The sediments that settled at the bottom of the seas were eroded from the terrestrial landscape. These sediments created what we now call Pictured Rocks,

Have an intimate experience with sandstone formations

which geologists terms call the Munising Formation.

The Munising Formation is made of several layers of rock, all having names that identify several popular attractions in the park. The top layer that the falls tumbles over is the younger and harder Au Train Formation. The next layer down is Miners Castle sandstone. Underneath is Chapel Rock sandstone. You can observe all three on this geological quest. Take a moment to feel the sands of time.

ACCESS

From Munising, take H-58 east to Sand Point Road, and turn left. Munising Falls Interpretive Center is on the right in less than a mile.

THE TRAIL

The trail leading up to the falls is paved asphalt that first snakes between an interpretive building (open during normal business hours) and a bathroom building. From here on, you will hike slightly uphill, paralleling Munising Creek. More notably, massive sandstone formations lunge upward on both sides of you, mostly obscured by the mature forest.

At just under 0.2 mile, you have reached the end of the trail, but not necessarily the end of the sights. An observation boardwalk at the terminus gives you a great perspective on the falls, cascading over sandstone millions of years in the making.

A staircase immediately to your right takes you up to a former access where visitors used to be able to walk behind the falls. With the erosion of the precipice, this has become a hazard, and this access has since been blocked. Only fools would walk out onto the slick sandstone, putting themselves at risk of sliding about 50 feet down onto a pile of rocks.

Back a couple hundred feet is another staircase that brings you up on the left side of the falls. Although the climb may make you feel old, consider that you are moving through time about a thousand years with every step. The sandstone is adjacent to the walkway, and you can run your hand against its grain, feeling sand fall away from this fragile stone.

On your way back to the parking area, take the time to identify some of the area's flora, such as the several varieties of ferns along the creek. In late spring and early summer, listen for woodland denizens like the ovenbird and its close, creekside-living relative, the northern waterthrush.

49

Grand Sable Falls

Place: Pictured Rocks National Lakeshore

Total distance: 2.4 miles round trip, or 0.2 mile (depending on where you park)

Hiking time: 1–1½ hours

Gradient: Mostly easy, 169-step staircase down to see falls

High points: Waterfall, backside of Grand Sable Dunes

Maps: USGS 7.5' Grand Sable Lake; NCT MI-10

Amenities: Visitor center, pit toilets

Footwear: Tennis shoes

Pets: Prohibited and illegal on trail, allowed in parking area

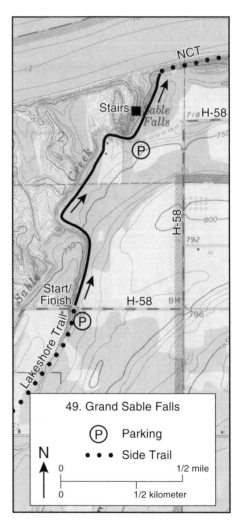

49. Grand Sable Falls

Ⓟ Parking

• • • Side Trail

N

0   1/2 mile

0   1/2 kilometer

SUMMARY

Grand Sable Falls is at the easternmost end of Pictured Rocks National Lakeshore. You would not expect this, since there are numerous falls at the west end of the national

Grand Sable Falls

lakeshore, and waterfalls get fewer and farther between as you head east.

You can park at the visitor center and take the clearly marked trail 1.2 miles to the falls. Alternatively, you can park at the falls, walk less than 0.1 mile to the top of the staircase, and proceed downward.

This trail shares a portion of the North Country Trail, which continues in both directions.

ACCESS

From Grand Marais, take H-58 west 1 mile to the falls parking lot, 2 miles to the visitor center. This is a modest visitor center compared to the one in Munising. There is ample parking, and bathrooms at each location.

THE TRAIL

Many backpackers begin or end their trips at the Grand Sable Visitor Center and pass on using the heavily wooded and lightly used trail to Grand Sable Falls. From the parking lot, there is a well-marked trailhead sign that takes you into mostly boreal woodlands.

Paralleling the Sable, you'll feel dwarfed passing through the forest. Keep your eyes peeled for striped maple, a boreal tree species. It doesn't grow much larger than an average person's forearm, but its alternating green and white stripes make it stand out from all the other vegetation.

It is not too evident, but you do skirt the backside of the Grand Sable Dunes rolling over the countryside. About 0.2 mile from the end, climb slightly.

This trail is part of the Grand Marais Ski Trail complex. Stay on track by following the North Country Trail and its markers. As you come to the three different ski loop intersections, take the paths most traveled, as the ski loops are used only in the winter and are not mowed or maintained in snowless months. The first is the "C" loop, then the "F" loop. The beginning of the "E" loop is at the top of the stairs going down to the falls.

Take the staircase down. There are a couple of overlooks as you descend into the gorge. At the bottom of the ravine, the boardwalk continues into the woods on the North Country Trail. Follow the trail to the river's mouth and Lake Superior. Turning east, the trail takes you to Woodland Beach, a large, private campground in Grand Marais, only 0.2 mile away. Since you made a significant decline in elevation, if you choose to climb to the top, you will have to gain that elevation back again, toiling up another staircase. You can make a loop back to the trailhead by using H-58.

Turning around and heading back up, you will be reminded that you descended 169 stair steps, which only means you have to climb them back to reach the top. When you stop to take a break, take in the mixed forest of balsam fir, striped maple, red maple, white spruce, speckled alder, and paper birch.

50

Sand Point

Place: Pictured Rocks National Lakeshore

Total distance: 0.5 mile

Hiking time: 1 hour

Gradient: Wheelchair accessible

High points: Interpretive trail in a rare wooded dune and swale habitat

Maps: USGS 7.5' Indiantown; NCT MI-10; interpretive brochure at trailhead

Amenities: picnic area, beach, pit toilets

Footwear: Flip-flops

Pets: Prohibited and illegal

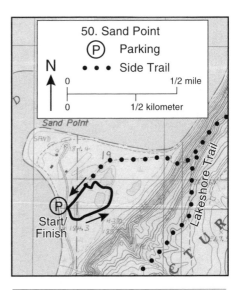

SUMMARY

If you cannot find the time to hike the entire 45-mile Lakeshore Trail, here is a chance for a much shorter stroll. Although it's only 0.5 mile, it will take you much longer to walk this boardwalk than you might think. Capturing your attention, the scenery is compliments of a rare habitat called wooded dune and swale. Sand ridges alternate with wetland depressions, allowing both dry, terrestrial plants and wetland plants to coexist only a few feet apart.

White pine and cedar are the common trees growing from the dry sand. Their lower brethren, sedges and lily pads, sprout from the cool waters. In the distance, look for a beaver lodge, but do not expect to find the beaver, unless you are there at dawn or dusk, as this is a crepuscular creature.

Wheelchair accessible boardwalk skirts between wetlands at Sand Point

Although you are walking a boardwalk about a hundred miles from the Lower Peninsula, this boardwalk has a Battle Creek connection, in that it was built with monies provided by the W.K. Kellogg Foundation.

As an added bonus, across the road is a spectacular view of Lake Superior and Grand Island, which is another hiking experience all its own (see Hike 41).

ACCESS

From the joint Hiawatha National Forest–Pictured Rocks National Lakeshore visitor center in Munising, turn right onto East Munising Avenue out of town. Turn left onto Sandpoint Road, which is marked with the large brown recreational highway signs. Take the road past Munising Falls and look for the beach parking on your left. The trailhead is directly across the road.

THE TRAIL

This wheelchair-accessible boardwalk not only attracts those less mobile, it also attracts those hard of sight, with its large-print, self-guiding brochure. Signs accompany the many benches and turnouts for viewing this interesting area.

Sand Point Trail is mostly boardwalk, but it starts out as a paved walkway. An advisory is posted that no pets are allowed on the boardwalk, and for good reason. Fido has nowhere to do his business if the urge arises other than on the boardwalk. In addition, there is a fair population of wildlife in the area, from squirrels to deer, and even beavers—plenty of opportunities for him to get into trouble.

Follow the boardwalk counterclockwise. It mostly stays to the sand ridges that alternate between the wetland areas, known as swales. On the ridges are mature white and red pines with an understory of lush blueberries and bracken fern.

The swales, where shallow, are dominated by spirea. Deeper pools are similar to a typical pond, with cattails around the edges and pond lily and spatterdock in the deeper pools. Tamaracks are sprinkled in for good measure.

Interpretive panels describe the area's ecology, wildlife, and geology. At the 0.4-mile mark, a large beaver pond and lodge dominate the landscape. If you look past the lodge, you will notice the forested escarpment thrusting into the sky. A panel describing the geology tells how where you are standing has settled from the surrounding landscape by several hundred feet. No, you are not in California—you are on a fault line, though!

The massive beaver lodge tells you that Michigan's largest rodent is nearby. Be careful in your identification, as muskrats look similar, at least in the water—but there is one major difference. Beavers have wide, flat tails and are not afraid to use them to startle you by slapping them against the water. Muskrats have naked, round tails. A small beaver looks like a large muskrat, so use your identification skills wisely.

Upon leaving the boardwalk, turn left on the paved trail and note the trailing arbutus on the forest floor. This uncommon plant is a favorite of botanists.

Sand Point

Appendix: List of Animals and Plants

ANIMALS

American redstart	*Setophaga ruticilla*
American robin	*Turdus americanus*
Bald eagle	*Haliaeetus leucocephalus*
Black bear	*Ursus americanus*
Beaver	*Castor canadensis*
Belted kingfisher	*Megaceryle alcyon*
Black-billed cuckoo	*Coccyzus erythropthalmus*
Black-capped chickadee	*Parus atricapillus*
Blackfly	*Simulium* spp.
Black-throated blue warbler	*Dendroica nigrescens*
Blue jay	*Cyanocitta cristata*
Bluegill	*Lepomis macrochirus*
Brown thrasher	*Toxostoma rufum*
Cedar waxwing	*Bombycilla cedrorum*
Common loon	*Gavia immer*
Common merganser	*Mergus merganser*
Common nighthawk	*Chordeiles minor*
Common yellowthroat	*Geothlypis trichas*
Coyote	*Canis latrans*
Deerfly	*Chrysops* spp.
Eastern kingbird	*Tyrannus tyrannus*
Eastern wood pewee	*Contopus virens*
Garter snake	*Thamnophis sirtalis*
Gray catbird	*Dumetella carolinensis*
Gray jay	*Perisoreus canadensis*
Great blue heron	*Ardea herodias*
Hairy woodpecker	*Picoides villosus*
Horsefly	*Tabanus* spp.
House wren	*Troglodytes aedon*
Least chipmunk	*Tamias minimus*
Least flycatcher	*Epidonax minimus*
Lynx	*Lynx canadensis*
Moose	*Alces alces*
Mosquito	*Aedes* spp.
Muskrat	*Ondatra zibethicus*
Northern shoveler	*Anas clypeata*

ANIMALS (cont.)

Northern waterthrush	*Seiurus noveboracensis*
Norway rat	*Rattus norvegicus*
No-see-um	Family *Ceratopogonidae*
Olive-sided flycatcher	*Nuttallornis borealis*
Osprey	*Pandion haliaetus*
Ovenbird	*Seiurus aurocapillus*
Painted turtle	*Chrysemys picta*
Pileated woodpecker	*Dryocopus pileatus*
Piping plover	*Charadrius melodus*
Porcupine	*Erethizon dorsatum*
Red fox	*Vulpes vulpes*
Red squirrel	*Sciurus vulgaris*
Red-breasted merganser	*Mergus serrator*
Red-eyed vireo	*Vireo olivaceus*
Red-winged blackbird	*Agelaius phoeniceus*
River otter	*Lontra canadensis*
Ruffed grouse	*Bonasa umbellus*
Sharp-shinned hawk	*Accipiter striatus*
Smallmouth bass	*Micropterus dolomieu*
Stable (beach) fly	*Stomoxys calcitrans*
Swamp sparrow	*Melospiza georgiana*
Walleye	*Sander vitreus vitreus*
White-breasted nuthatch	*Sitta carolinensis*
White-tailed deer	*Odocoileus virginianus*
White-throated sparrow	*Zonotrichia albicollis*
Winter wren	*Troglodytes troglodytes*
Wolf	*Canis lupus*
Yellow-rumped warbler	*Dendroica coronata*

HABITATS

For more information, see "Michigan's Natural Communities" at the Michigan State University Extension Web site: http://web4.msue.msu.edu/mnfi/data/MNFI_Natural_Communities.pdf.

Bedrock beach	Interdunal wetland
Bedrock glade	Mesic northern forest
Bog	Muskeg
Boreal	Northern hardwood forest
Cobble beach	Open dunes
Dry northern forest	Sand beach
Dry-mesic northern forest	Wooded dune and swale
Great Lakes barren	

Appendix

PLANTS

American ginseng	*Panax quinquefolium*
American (Canada) yew	*Taxus canadensis*
American beech	*Fagus grandifolia*
Balsam fir	*Abies balsamea*
Balsam poplar	*Populus balsamifera*
Basswood	*Tilia americana*
Beak-rush	*Eleocharis* spp.
Bearberry	*Arctostaphylos uva-ursi*
Black ash	*Fraxinus nigra*
Black cherry	*Prunus serotina*
Black spruce	*Picea mariana*
Bloodroot	*Sanguinaria canadensis*
Blue flag iris	*Iris palustris*
Blue-beech	*Carpinus caroliniana*
Blueberry	*Vaccinium* spp.
Bracken fern	*Pteridium aquilinum*
Braun's holly fern	*Polystichum braunii*
Bull thistle	*Cirsium vulgare*
Bulrush	*Scirpus* spp.
Bunchberry	*Cornus canadensis*
Burdock	*Arctium* spp.
Butterwort	*Pinguicula* spp.
Calamovilfa (sandreed)	*Calamovilfa* spp.
Canada mayflower	*Maianthemum canadense*
Cattail	*Typha* spp.
Cinnamon fern	*Osmunda cinnamomea*
Cinquefoil	*Potentilla* spp.
Clintonia (blue bead lily)	*Clintonia borealis*
Clubmoss	*Lycopodium* spp.
Common polypody	*Polypodium virginianum*
Dogwood	*Cornus* spp.
Doll's eyes	*Actaea pachypoda*
Dwarf primrose	*Primula mistassinica*
Elderberry	*Sambucus nigra canadensis*
Evergreen woodfern	*Dryopteris intermedia*
False Solomon's seal	*Smilacina racemosa*
Fireweed	*Chamerion angustifolium*
Fringed polygala	*Polygala paucifolia*
Garlic mustard	*Alliaria petiolata*
Hairy goldenrod	*Solidago hispida*
Heart-leaved Arnica	*Arnica cordifolia*
Horsetail	*Equisetum* spp.
Houghton's goldenrod	*Oligoneuron houghtonii*

PLANTS (cont.)

Ironwood (American hop-hornbeam)	*Ostrya virginiana*
Jewelweed	*Impatiens capensis*
Lake Huron iris (dwarf lake iris)	*Iris lacustris*
Large-leafed aster	*Eurybia macrophylla*
Large-toothed aspen	*Populus grandidentata*
Leatherleaf	*Chamaedaphne* spp.
Liverwort	*Marchantiophyta* spp.
Lobelia	*Lobelia* spp.
Lombardy poplar	*Populus nigra*
Low sweet blueberry	*Vaccinium angustifolium*
Maidenhair fern	*Adiantum pedatum*
Marsh bellflower	*Campanula aparinoides*
Marsh grass of Parnassus	*Parnassia palustris*
Mountain ash	*Sorbus americana*
Ninebark	*Physocarpus opulifolius*
Northern hemlock	*Tsuga canadensis*
Oak fern	*Gymnocarpium dryopteris*
Ohio goldenrod	*Oligoneuron ohioense*
Ostrich fern	*Matteuccia struthiopteris*
Pale painted cup (Indian paintbrush)	*Castilleja septentrionalis*
Panic grass	*Panicum* spp.
Paper birch	*Betula papyrifera*
Phragmities	*Phragmites australis*
Pink lady's slipper (moccasin flower)	*Cypripedium acaule*
Poison ivy	*Toxicodendron radicans*
Poison sumac	*Toxicodendron vernix*
Polypody fern (Christmas fern)	*Polystichum acrostichoides*
Poplar	*Populus tremuloides*
Purple cliff-brake	*Pellaea atropurpurea*
Pyrola	*Pyrola* spp.
Queen Anne's lace (wild carrot)	*Daucus carota*
Raspberry	*Rubus* spp.
Red elderberry	*Sambucus racemosa*
Red maple	*Acer rubrum*
Red oak	*Quercus rubra*
Red pine	*Pinus resinosa*
Rose twisted-stalk	*Streptopus lanceolatus*
Rue anemone (purple rue)	*Thalictrum dasycarpum*
Rusty woodsia	*Woodsia ilvensis*
Sarsaparilla	*Aralia nudicaulis*
Sedge	*Carex* spp.
Sensitive fern	*Onoclea sensibilis*
Silverweed	*Argentina anserina*

PLANTS (cont.)

Smaller fringed gentian	*Gentianopsis virgata*
Small-flowered gerardia (false foxglove)	*Agalinis paupercula*
Solomon's seal	*Polygonatum* spp.
Spatterdock (yellow pond lily)	*Nuphar lutea*
Speckled alder	*Alnus incana*
Sphagnum moss	*Sphagnum* spp.
Spirea	*Spirea alba*
Spleenwort	*Asplenium* spp.
Staghorn sumac	*Rhus typhina*
Starflower	*Trientalis borealis*
Striped maple	*Acer pensylvanicum*
Sugar maple	*Acer saccharum*
Swamp rose	*Rosa palustris*
Sweet cicely	*Osmorhiza berteroi*
Sweetgale	*Myrica gale*
Tamarack	*Larix laricina*
Three-leafed goldthread	*Coptis trifolia*
Trailing arbutus	*Epigaea repens*
Trillium	*Trillium* spp.
Velvetleaf blueberry(huckleberry)	*Vaccinium myrtilloides*
Violet	*Viola* spp.
Walking fern	*Asplenium rhizophyllum*
White ash	*Fraxinus americana*
White baneberry	*Actaea pachypoda*
White cedar	*Thuja occidentalis*
White pine	*Pinus strobus*
White spruce	*Picea glauca*
White water lily	*Nymphaea odorata*
Willow	*Salix* spp.
Wintergreen	*Gaultheria procumbens*
Yarrow	*Achillea millefolium*
Yellow birch	*Betula alleghaniensis*
Yellow lady's slipper	*Cypripedium parviflorum*

Resources and Bibliography

Rollin Baker. *Michigan Mammals*. East Lansing, MI: Michigan State University Press, 1980.

Burton V. Barnes and Warren H. Wagner. *Michigan Trees: A Guide to the Trees of Michigan and the Great Lakes Region*. Ann Arbor, MI: The University of Michigan Press. 1981.

Tom Carney. *Natural Wonders of Michigan*. New York: McGraw-Hill, 1999.

Steve Chadde. *A Great Lakes Wetland Flora*. Laurium, MI: Pocket Flora Press. 2002.

Boughton Cobb, Elizabeth Farnsworth, and Cheryl Lowe. 2005. *Peterson's Guide to Ferns*. Boston, New York: Houghton Mifflin, 2005.

John A. Dorr and Donald F. Eschman. *Geology of Michigan*. Ann Arbor, MI: The University of Michigan Press, 1970.

Jim DuFresne. *Michigan State Parks*. Seattle, WA: The Mountaineers, 1989.

Arthur V. Evans. *Field Guide to Insects and Spiders of North America*. New York: Sterling Publications, 2007.

Dennis R. Hansen. *Trail Atlas of Michigan* (3rd Edition). Okemos, MI: Hansen Publishing Company, 2002.

James Harding. *Michigan Snakes*. East Lansing, MI: Michigan State University Press, 1991.

James Harding and J. Alan Holman. *Michigan Turtles and Lizards*. East Lansing, MI: Michigan State University Press. 1992.

James Harding and J. Alan Homan. *Michigan Frogs, Toads, and Salaman-* ders. East Lansing, MI: Michigan State University Press, 1993.

John Kricher and Gordon Morrison. *Peterson Field Guide: Eastern Forests*. Boston, New York: Houghton Mifflin Company, 1988.

Allen Kurta. *Mammals of the Great Lakes Region*. Ann Arbor, MI: University of Michigan Press, 2005.

Michigan Natural Features Inventory. *Michigan Natural Community Types*. Michigan State University Extension, 2006. Retrieved from http://web4.msue.msu.edu/mnfi/data/MNFI_Natural_Communities.pdf.

Lawrence Newcomb. *Newcomb's Wildflower Guide*. Boston: Little, Brown, and Company, 1989.

Bill and Laurie Penrose. *A Guide to 199 Michigan Waterfalls*. Davidons, MI: Friede Publications, 1988.

Roger Tory Peterson. *Eastern Birds* (4th Edition). Boston, New York: Houghton Mifflin Company, 1980.

Ann and Myron Sutton. *Eastern Forests*. New York: Chanticleer Press, 1985.

Stat Tekiela. *Wildflowers of Michigan*. Cambridge, MN: Adventure Publications, Inc., 2000.

Universal Map Company. *Michigan Recreational Travel Atlas*. Williamston, MI: Universal Map Enterprises, 2007.

Edward G. Voss. *Michigan Flora* (Volumes I, II, III). Bloomfield Hills, MI: Cranbrook Institute of Science,1972.

Joe Walewski. *Lichens of the North Woods*. Duluth, MN: Kollath and Stensaas Publishing, 2007.

Index

S

T

U

Union, 187
Union Bay Campground, 61
Universal Oil Company, 33
Upper Tahquamenon Falls, 125, 158, 170,
    172, 173, 174
USFS 326, 103
USFS 400, 104
USFS 630, 105
USFS 642, 106

V

Valley Trail, 80
Van Riper State Park, 94, 111, 113
Victoria, 102, 106
Victoria Dam, 106
Victoria Road, 105, 106
Voyageur II, 43

W

Wakefield, 56
War of 1812, 149
Water Tank Lakes, 128
Watersmeet, 90
weather, 18–19, 21–22
Wells, Walter, 84
Wells State Park, 84
West Chickenbone Campground, 44, 45
West Rim Trail, 196
West Shore-East Shore Trails (Presque
    Isle River Loop) hike
        getting there, 56
        hike overview, 54
        map, 55
        trail description, 56–57
Whiskey Hollow Creek, 106
White Pine, 103
White Pine Mine, 67–68
White Pine Trail, 180, 181
Whitefish Bay, 176
Whitefish Lake, 91
Whitefish Point Bird Observatory, 175,
    176, 177
Whitefish Point hike
    getting there, 175
    hike overview, 175
    map, 176
    trail description, 176–78
Whittier Trail, 117

wild sarsaparilla, 86
Williams Landing, 196
Windigo, 40, 42, 43
winter wren, 122
winterberry, 30–31
W. K. Kellogg Foundation, 225
wolf, 40, 42, 96
wooded dune and swale habitat, 223
Woodland Beach, 222
Woods Trail, 70